SEVENTH EDITION

TriLog

Diary and Guide for the Triathlete

TIM HOUTS

Mc
Graw
Hill

New York   Chicago   San Francisco   Lisbon   London   Madrid   Mexico City
Milan   New Delhi   San Juan   Seoul   Singapore   Sydney   Toronto

Library of Congress Cataloging-in-Publication Data

Houts, Tim.
    Trilog : diary and guide for the triathlete / Tim Houts. — 7th ed.
        p. cm.
    ISBN-13: 978-0-07-159780-7 (alk. paper)
    ISBN-10: 0-07-159780-8 (alk. paper)
    1. Triathlon—Training—Forms. I. Title. II. Title: Tri log.
    GV1060.73.H68   2008
    796.42'57—dc22

                                                2008005163

4 5 6 7 8 9 10 QVS 16 15

ISBN 978-0-07-159780-7
MHID   0-07-159780-8

Interior design by Think Design Group LLC
Interior photographs copyright © 2007 by Rich Cruse/richcruse.com

McGraw-Hill books are available at special quantity discounts to use as premiums and sales promotions or for use in corporate training programs. To contact a representative, please visit the Contact Us pages at www.mhprofessional.com.

This book is printed on acid-free paper.

Contents

Introduction

Welcome to *TriLog*, a tool to help you turn your triathlon and fitness goals into reality! By using this log, you've already taken the first step on your training journey. Somebody once said, "If you don't know where you're going, how can you expect to get there?" Kind of funny, but true!

TriLog will help you map your training destination and track your progress along the way, so if you get detoured, you can get back on track. Not only will you know where you want to go, but you'll know whether the path you've taken is moving you in the right direction, and you'll know when you get there.

We hope you enjoy *TriLog*'s features:

Training Guide

This 36-page guide provides some training basics like workout organization, goal setting, and progression, as well as several sample workouts that can provide a starting point for the beginner to the advanced triathlete.

Easy-to-Use Diary Pages

In this edition, I've taken time to make the easy-to-use diary pages even better. The pages still give you plenty of room to note your workouts, whether swimming, biking, or running. But I've also added a section to note your hydration, fueling, and any other comments. And I've freshened up the page design to add a little more visual interest. I hope these pages help take you where you want to go!

Motivational Photos

As in previous editions, a host of remarkable photos throughout the book will inspire, motivate, and help you to keep your training on track all the way to your training and racing goals.

Train well. Eat well. Live great!

PART 1
Training Guide

Swimming Intervals and Sets

To get the most from your swim training, break your swim workouts into *sets* of *swims* repeated on fixed *intervals*. *Swims* are described by distance, stroke, and focus (e.g., "100-yard freestyle" [4 laps of 25 yards]). *Sets* are groups of swims within a workout. (Swimming 100 yards 10 times is a *set of ten 100s*, or *10 × 100*.) *Intervals* are the times you start each swim in a set. For an interval of 2:00 (two minutes), you start a new swim each time the clock hits 2:00 (as in 10 × 100 @ 2:00).

Choose your intervals in a set to give enough rest so you can hold your *repeat time* (the time it takes you to finish the swim) throughout the set. Adjust your intervals according to your conditioning, where you are in your training season. Push yourself while maintaining proper swim technique.

Give yourself extra rest during warm-up and less rest during main sets. For example, one day a set of 3 × 200s may be your warm-up set on an interval of 4:30, while another day a set of 8 × 200s may be your main set on an interval of 3:30 or 3:45.

Swim Quality, Not Quantity

Remember that the swim leg is the shortest of the three legs of the triathlon. So keep in mind that your goal is to get the most out of your swim workouts without taking too much time away from your cycling and running workouts. Work up to swimming 2,000 to 3,000 yards per workout, two to three times per week, to get ready for a 1.5K swim leg.

Pick Your Sets

In planning your workout, pick one or two main sets to be the focus. Place them after your warm-up set(s). Remember to mix in different sets to your workouts so you never swim the same set twice during any week. This will help keep your workouts interesting and minimize boredom.

Here are some common swim sets you can use:

Mid-Distance or Power Sets

Sets of 200s to 400s (200 to 400 yards) are great mid-distance sets that can help you develop strength and endurance. These power sets will allow you to swim your swim leg at a pace close to your 100 repeat times. Use these sets often as your main set. Pick a repeat interval based on your 100 interval. For example, if your interval for a set of 100s is 2:00, then try your 200s on a 4:00 interval, your 300s on 6:00, and your 400s on 8:00.

Following are examples of power sets:

8 × 200 @ 4:00

5 × 300 @ 6:00

4 × 400 @ 8:00

2 × 400 @ 8:00, 2 × 300 @ 6:00, 2 × 200 @ 4:00

Sprint Sets

Sprint sets of shorter swims, such as 25s (25 yards), 50s, and 100s, will help develop speed, strength, and anaerobic capacity.

Pick your intervals for your sprint sets to allow you 5 to 25 seconds of rest between swims. Put your sprint sets toward the end of your workout so you'll be fully warmed up. Do 4 to 12 swims per sprint set.

Following are examples of sprint sets:

10 × 25 @ :30

8 × 50 @ 1:00

10 × 100 @ 2:00

Pyramid Sets

Use pyramid sets to add variety and difficulty to your workouts. To create a pyramid set, (1) start with shorter swims; (2) build increments to longer swims; (3) decrease the same increments back to your starting swim distance.

An example of a pyramid set is 1 × 50 @ 1:00, 1 × 100 @ 2:00, 1 × 200 @ 4:00, 1 × 300 @ 6:00, 1 × 400 @ 8:00, 1 × 300 @ 6:00, 1 × 200 @ 4:00, 1 × 100 @ 2:00, and finally, 1 × 50 @ 1:00. This pyramid totals 1,700 yards.

Kickboard, Paddle, Pull Buoy, and Fin Sets

Kickboards, paddles, and other accessories can help you strengthen specific parts of your swim stroke. Use hand paddles and pull buoys occasionally in mid-distance sets to improve arm stroke strength, provide workout variety, and give you a better feel for pulling through the water.

Use kickboard sets to increase kick strength. A couple of 100- to 200-yard kicking sets should be plenty per workout.

Use swim fins occasionally in kicking sets and in sprint swim sets to build anaerobic capacity, add workout variety, and feel what it is like to swim really, really fast.

One final tip: to get the greatest swim training results, work out with a Masters swim club or with a coach to improve your stroke and to be pushed harder.

Sample Workouts

Here are a few sample workouts (freestyle, unless noted):

WORKOUT 1

1 × 300	Warm-up
2 × 50 @ :45–1:00	More warm-up, increase speed through set
1 × 100	Kicking
5 × 200 @ 3:00–4:00	Main set; feel a strong, steady pace
1 × 100	Cooldown

Workout total: 2,200 yards

WORKOUT 2

1 × 500	Warm-up
1 × 200	Kicking
1 × 1,700	Main set; pyramid (see example)
1 × 100	Kicking
4 × 50 @ 1:00–1:15	Work hard, set interval to give plenty of rest
1 × 50	Cooldown

Workout total: 2,750 yards

WORKOUT 3

1 × 400	Reverse IM (individual medley) as warm-up
6 × 50 @ :45–1:15	More warm-up; increase speed through set
5 × 300 @ 4:30–6:00	Main set; get stronger through set
1 × 250	Kicking
5 × 100 @ 1:30–2:15	Hold repeat times consistent
1 × 50	Cooldown

Workout total: 3,000 yards

Open Water Swimming

Open water swims can provide you a break from lap swimming in the pool and can help prepare you for race day's open water swim. Find an open water course you can swim once a week to develop a feel for swimming and navigating open water.

Safety Precautions

In the right conditions, open water swimming can be one of the most enjoyable parts of your training. But it's also one that deserves some attention to safety. Remember these basics safety tips: Swim with a partner. Survey the water for prevailing conditions such as wind, surf, currents, and any other hazards before entering. Ask your lifeguard, Masters swim coach, or other local expert for advice on open water swimming in your area.

Swim Straight

There's a reason they have lane lines and a painted line at the bottom of most training pools: they help you swim straight. It's a breath of fresh air to get away from those lines when you swim in open water, but it also makes swimming a straight course harder. On each leg of your swim, locate a landmark such as a buoy, a raft, or a point on shore to aim for and lift your head every several strokes to see that you're still on course. Adjust your course as needed. Learning to swim a straight course (which is the shortest course) is the easiest way to a faster time.

Sample Open Water Swim Workouts

Workout 1: Parallel Swim

In the ocean, a lake, or a bay, swim 10 to 25 strokes out from the beach (or just outside the surf line), then swim parallel to the shore for a quarter to a half mile. Then swim back. Be sure to swim with a partner. Swimming close to shore will make you feel more comfortable your first few times in open water. Try to increase your speed for the second half of your swim.

Workout 2: In and Outs

To warm up, swim 50 to 60 percent of your normal course. Then find a starting point on the beach and a buoy (real or imagined) 50 to 200 yards offshore. Run into the water and swim out, round the buoy, and back to your starting point on the beach. Repeat two to five times. Concentrate on swimming a straight line to and from the buoy. Get comfortable entering and exiting the water and going through the surf (if any). Ask the lifeguard or a fellow open water swimmer to give you tips on how best to get in and out of the water or through the surf.

Workout 3: Swim-Run-Swims

Do the same as Workout 2, but incorporate a 200- to 400-yard beach run between swim sets to create a swim-run-swim course. (Or do a run-swim-run course.) Get comfortable in the water and have fun!

Cycling Endurance and Power

The bike leg is the longest of the three triathlon legs. As a result, by improving your bike time you give yourself the greatest opportunity to make the biggest overall time gains. Your cycling endurance base is the foundation for all other types of cycling training such as intervals, power work, and hills. Endurance is the easiest to build: it comes from spending enough time in the saddle on the road. The big question is, how much endurance training do you need before moving on to power, hills, and speed?

Endurance Training

Look at the lengths of your events to figure how much endurance work you need. Work up to, and mix in, distances of 75 percent, 100 percent, and 150 percent of the event distances. For example, work in rides of 20, 25, and 40 miles of endurance in preparation for an Olympic distance race with a 40K bike (approximately 25 miles).

The endurance-building process should extend over one to two months, and during that time you should avoid speed or intensity training. Once you have a solid endurance base you can reduce your pure endurance work as you incorporate other types of training rides, since maintaining endurance training takes less effort than building it.

Quality, Not Quantity

More is not necessarily better. Sometimes cyclists feel that if they ride greater distances, almost to the point of punishment, they'll automatically become better and faster. But that's not true. All you'll get out of a consistent overabundance of endurance miles is slow legs, slower reaction time, and a lower top speed.

Don't waste energy overtraining in one area that you could be using for other areas, like swimming, running, strength training, or speed work. A couple of huge rides here and there never really hurt, but don't do them to the exclusion of higher quality intensity training that puts the edge on your form.

Sample Endurance Workouts

Here is a sample week of endurance workouts. The distances mentioned are relative to your event bike leg distance and to your conditioning as you move through your early season period of building endurance:

Monday: Long-distance ride, easy

Tuesday: Medium ride

Wednesday: Cycling day off

Thursday: Short ride

Friday: Cycling day off

Saturday: Long ride

Sunday: Medium ride or cycling day off

Training for Power

Power on the bike is the ability to maintain momentum in short bursts through tough spots on a ride, such as headwinds, short hills, sudden accelerations, and rolling terrain.

The best way to train to build power is to do plain, hard rides, but with more focus on maintaining momentum and pedaling smoothly. A great way to build power is to ride with someone of equal or greater fitness than you who can push you as you try to maintain pace.

In a power workout, warm up first while riding to a familiar section of relatively uninterrupted road. After the warm-up, try to maintain a constant effort of about 85 to 95 percent. (A heart rate monitor is great, but good old intuition works nearly as well too.) Try to keep your pedal cadence at a steady 80 to 90 RPM. Use slightly more difficult gearing than you might normally use to help build power.

Remember to focus on finesse when pedaling a more difficult gear during power training. Finesse the pedals, don't mash them; think "circular" and "smooth." You'll be surprised at how difficult a gear you can maintain. But if you find yourself struggling, try an easier gear; it's better to be smooth.

Concentrate on building controlled power and momentum, not speed. Focus on tempo, like a metronome: constant, smooth, strong pedaling. Keep your effort and speed smooth and even through the difficult sections of your training course. It's easier to maintain your momentum by working harder for short periods than it is to regain it. That's power.

Sample Power Workouts

Here is a sample week of bike training incorporating power workouts:

Monday: Medium-distance ride

Tuesday: Power ride on flat terrain

Wednesday: Cycling day off

Thursday: Long ride

Friday: Cycling day off

Saturday: Power ride on rolling terrain

Sunday: Medium-distance easy ride or cycling day off

Cycling Speed

ntervals are a way to organize your workouts into repeated efforts that focus on building speed. While shorter intervals can help cycling road racers in their race situations, longer cycling intervals will help you develop speed more suited to triathlon and duathlon (essentially time trials against the clock, not other cyclists). Be sure to build a solid base of four to six weeks of cycling endurance training and two to four weeks of cycling power training before incorporating any interval work into your training.

Find a course for your intervals that is flat, slightly downhill, or mildly rolling. Do your intervals with a tailwind if possible, since you're trying to develop speed, not power or strength.

Intervals

Design your intervals to be at least two minutes and as long as 10 miles. Any longer, and you'll be building power. Do fewer intervals as you increase their distance. For example, you might do 10 two-minute intervals or two 10-mile intervals. Ride easy between intervals to recover completely, with breathing controlled, heart rate back to normal, and mind ready for another intense effort.

Interval Workouts

Use these workouts to develop your speed:

2-Minute/5-Minute Intervals

Use a 15- to 30-minute ride to your interval course as warm-up. Then, for your first interval, ride all out for 2 minutes. Ride easy as you recover before your next interval. Repeat for a total of four 2-minute intervals. Follow this set of intervals with a set of two 5-minute intervals. Recover fully, then do two 2-minute intervals. Recover fully, then do two 5-minute intervals; recover; do one 5-minute interval. Cool down with a 15-minute easy ride.

5-Minute/2-Mile Intervals

Use a 15- to 30-minute ride to your interval course as warm-up. Then, ride all out for a 5-minute interval. Ride easy between intervals to recover fully. Repeat for four 5-minute intervals. Follow with a set of 2-mile intervals. Recover between. Repeat for a total of two 2-mile intervals. Cool down with a 15-minute easy ride.

10-Mile Intervals

Use a 15- to 30-minute ride to your interval course as warm-up. Ride with 100 percent effort for a 10-mile interval. Concentrate on speed. Your slightly downhill course will help you maintain fast MPH and RPM through the entire interval. Ride easy to recover fully between intervals. Then repeat for a total of two 10-mile intervals. Cool down with a 15-minute easy ride.

Sample Week with Speed Workouts

Here is a sample week of training with speed workouts:

Monday: Medium-distance ride

Tuesday: Power ride on flat terrain

Wednesday: Cycling day off

Thursday: 5-minute/2-mile intervals

Friday: Cycling day off

Saturday: 2-minute/5-minute intervals

Sunday: 10-mile intervals or cycling day off

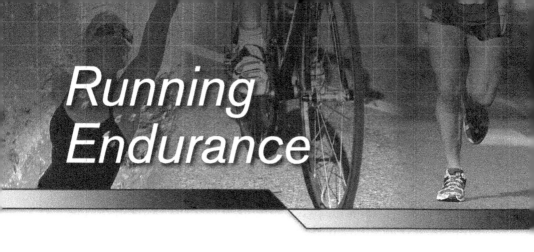

Running Endurance

Endurance training is the first of three training steps to a faster triathlon running leg. It's the conditioning base on which two other training steps, strength and speed, are built.

Although the endurance stage of training may be the easiest to attain, it's also the most important. Without a solid foundation of at least three to five weeks of endurance training, strength or speed training will offer minimal performance returns and may instead lead to injury.

Run Relaxed

Master the art of running relaxed during your endurance training runs: (1) keep your wrists and hands loose; (2) run with your thumbs up and elbows in, close to your side, to prevent your arms from tightening up; (3) relax your lower jaw, feeling it move up and down with each stride; and (4) run "tall" with your hips slightly forward without any forward lean, keeping your feet under your body as you maintain a good stride.

Set Your Distance

As a general rule, build up to running your shorter endurance runs at about 75 percent of your event distance and your longer endurance runs at about 125 percent of event distance. For example, if you're training for a 10K (6.2 miles), make your shorter endurance runs four to five miles and longer ones seven to nine miles.

Adjust your training distances to your fitness level as it changes throughout your training season. Run shorter distances early in the season and longer distances as you make progress with your training. Limit your mileage increases to less than 10 percent per week to prevent injury and overtraining. For example, if you ran 20 miles one week, adding 10 percent would increase your mileage to 22 miles the next.

Alternate your long runs with medium or short runs to help your body recover from previous training and to help you stay fresh mentally and physically.

Set Your Pace

Set your training pace to one that you can maintain throughout your run. Find a pace that allows you to run loose and tall. Adjust your pace to your fitness level as it changes throughout your training season; a pace that's too fast at the beginning of the season may be too slow at the end.

Remember that in endurance training, pace is less important than distance.

Run your slow endurance runs at about 50 percent of your race pace, your medium endurance runs at about 70 percent of race pace, and your fast endurance runs at about 85 percent of race pace. Refer to the Running Training and Race Pace Chart in this book to see what your training pace might look like. Additionally, if you use a heart rate monitor, you can note your corresponding heart rates at these effort levels and use your HR monitor to help you stay at your goal pace.

Mix It Up

Incorporate different courses into your endurance training (and all of your training). Find at least five different courses to mix into your running routine to keep you mentally and physically fresh.

Choose a variety of running surfaces to help prevent injury. Find routes that take you on grass, sand, or dirt trails as alternatives to running every day on cement sidewalks or asphalt roads.

Be creative in designing your courses. Include loop, out-and-back, and point-to-point runs. Mix in courses with hills, gentle slopes, scenery, curves, straights, and flats. Have fun with your runs! Isn't that what it's all about anyway?

Sample Week of Endurance Training

Here's an example of how to put together a week of training to focus on endurance:

Monday: Do a short, easy run. Stay relaxed and comfortable.

Tuesday: Go medium distance. Remember to run tall and relaxed.

Wednesday: Running day off.

Thursday: Put in a medium-distance run. Get in the groove and lose yourself in the run. Mix in a different course.

Friday: Make it a long, slow run. Don't worry about pace. Try to go an extra mile or two. Have a running partner join you for a portion, or all, of your long run.

Saturday: Put in a short run. Stay loose and enjoy it.

Sunday: Day off. Let your body recover and rejuvenate itself.

Running for Strength

Training to build strength and conditioning is the second step to a faster time and better finish. It bridges the training gap between endurance and speed training. Build a base of three to five weeks of endurance training before mixing strength workouts into your training.

Running for strength improves your overall running ability by putting power and strength into your stride. This added power will help you push through training runs, run relaxed during races, and maintain pace up hills and into wind. Additionally, strength running builds upper leg power that provides for a longer, more efficient stride, which means that a runner who runs for strength as well as endurance can always beat a runner who only runs for endurance.

The two main types of strength running workouts are (1) hills and stairs and (2) fartleks.

Maintain Form on Hills and Stairs

Concentrate on maintaining good running form more than pace to get the most out of running hills and stairs. Remember, this is strength running work, not speed work (which you'll do later on the track).

Set your pace so you'll be tired at the end of the workout but not exhausted. Concentrate on good running form. Visualize it. Drive your knees up and pump your arms on every stride. Run tall and dive off the balls of your feet. Adjust your running form to meet the hill or stair. Shorten your stride and increase your tempo.

Choose Your Hills and Stairs

You can run hills and stairs two ways: (1) hill or stair repeats or
(2) hill circuits. Choose the workouts according to what you have
available. Mix up your hill and stair workouts to keep you fresh
and to prevent injury.

Sample Hill and Stair Workout

Here are examples of hill and stair workouts. Use these as guidelines for your workouts. Adjust your runs to your fitness level as
it changes throughout your training.

HILL REPEATS

1. Find a steep hill, approximately 15 percent gradient, almost
   as steep as a flight of stairs in your home.
2. Warm up with a one- to two-mile easy run.
3. Run 300 meters up the hill. Remember to focus on good
   running form, not speed.
4. Walk or jog slowly down the hill to prevent knee injury.
5. Repeat 8 to 12 times.
6. Cool down with a one- to two-mile easy run.

STAIRS

1. Find a nearby school with a stadium or set of outdoor stairs
   that can accommodate your workouts.
2. Run to the top of the stairs. Again, concentrate on your running
   form, not pace; keep your knees up and pump your arms.
3. Be careful as you walk or jog down the stairs.
4. Repeat for a 15-minute set. (The number of runs you do to the
   top of the stairs in that time will depend on the height of the
   stairs.)

HILL CIRCUITS

1. Find a medium-distance run that includes a series of several
   hills.
2. Design your course to take you through at least one to two
   miles of flat terrain as a warm-up before you come to any hills.
3. Run up and jog down your first hill, then move on to the next
   one.

4. Repeat for 7 to 10 hills.

5. Include a one- to two-mile cooldown after the hills. Find a course you can use repeatedly.

Fartleks

Fartleks are another running strength workout. Fartleks are training runs that include periods of hard, then easy intervals in a continuous run. They will give you the strength to accelerate as needed to adjust to pace changes in a race and also teach your body tempo and rhythm.

During the hard fartlek intervals, accelerate to 75 to 80 percent of your race pace and concentrate on running tall, smooth, and strong. Remember that this is strength running work, not speed work, so don't sprint or race. Control and maintain this moderately fast pace.

During the easy fartlek intervals, focus on running relaxed, slow, and loose. Run as slow as 30 percent of your race pace. Catch your breath with long, slow, deep breaths and recover fully in preparation for the next hard interval. Shorten your easy/recovery intervals as you move through your training season and improve your conditioning.

Use the timer feature on a digital watch (with the repeat function on) to keep track of your hard/easy intervals.

Sample Fartlek Workouts

Use the following fartlek examples as a guideline of how to build strength into your stride and put a bound into your step.

TWO-MINUTE FARTLEK

1. Find an easy, open course.

2. Warm up with an easy one-mile run.

3. While running, accelerate into a two-minute hard run; control your pace and run smooth.

4. Run two minutes easy; recover and run loose.

5. Repeat this hard/easy fartlek for 30 minutes.

6. Cool down with a one-mile easy run.

PYRAMID FARTLEK
1. Find an easy, open course.
2. Warm up with an easy one-mile run.
3. Run 15 seconds hard, followed by 15 seconds easy.
4. Run 30 seconds hard, followed by 30 seconds easy.
5. Increase by 15 seconds each hard/easy interval until you reach two-minute intervals. When your training level allows, follow this increasing side of the pyramid back down by decreasing the interval times by 15 seconds from two minutes until you get back to your starting point of 15-second intervals.
6. Cool down with an easy one-mile run.

Sample Week of Running for Strength

Here's a sample week of training that shows how to incorporate strength runs with your endurance runs.

Monday: Go on a long-distance run. Relax, stay comfortable, and enjoy it.

Tuesday: Run a medium hill circuit, about 90 to 100 percent of race distance. Maintain form up the hills and run strong.

Wednesday: Running day off.

Thursday: Do a two-minute fartlek run. Remember to run tall and smooth.

Friday: Run long and easy. Lose yourself in the run and stay relaxed.

Saturday: Run 10 to 15 minutes of stairs, followed by a very short run of 40 to 50 percent of race distance.

Sunday: Day off. Give your body a chance to rest and recover.

Running Speed Work

Speed work is the third step, the icing on your training cake, to a faster race and better finish. You'll put the finishing touches on your endurance and strength workouts with three to five weeks of speed training. Speed work will give you an extra gear to shift into during races or training duels.

Although speed work can give you the ability to crank out personal records, it's also the cause of many running injuries. Consider doing speed work only after building a training foundation of endurance and strength. Only with this foundation can speed work be effective and safe.

Warm-Up Is Key

To prevent injuries and increase your performance, warm up and stretch thoroughly before you run any speed work. Run at least one to two miles easy as a warm-up. Pay special attention to your stretching before and after speed work.

Set Your Distances

Speed work teaches your body that it can run faster by *running it faster*. Run it faster by running shorter distances at a faster pace. Decrease the length and increase the pace of your intervals as your conditioning improves through your training season and your race date nears. Run shorter, faster intervals two to three weeks prior to your race to help you peak.

Set Your Intervals

As a general rule, run your intervals at a pace faster than your race pace. This teaches your body that it *can* run faster than your race pace. But the key to getting the most out of your speed work is to run your intervals at just the right level above your race pace. Running too fast will lead to injury, and running too slow will limit improvement.

Use the following as target ranges for your speed work intervals:

1-mile intervals: 3 to 5 percent faster than race pace

800-meter (half-mile) intervals: 8 to 10 percent faster than race pace

400-meter (quarter-mile) intervals: 10 to 12 percent faster than race pace

200-meter (eighth-mile) intervals: 12 to 15 percent faster than race pace

For example, if you run a 10K at 40:00, that's a 6:22 race pace per mile. Your interval goal time to complete a 1-mile interval would be 6:00–6:10 (3–5 percent faster).

Adjust your interval pace to your conditioning level as it changes throughout your training season. Refer to the Running Interval Training Pace Chart in this guide to find your intervals pace. And remember, run hard and fast, but run controlled.

Set Your Recovery

Set your recovery times and distances so you can maintain consistent times throughout your workout, but not long enough for you to get cold between intervals.

As a general rule, to recover between intervals, walk or jog easy half the distance of the interval being run. Limit your recovery to less than five minutes to prevent an unintended cooldown.

Sample Speed Workouts

Here are sample speed workouts. Remember: adjust your interval and recovery times according to your changing fitness level.

MILE INTERVALS

1. Stretch and warm up completely with an easy one-mile run.
2. Run four 1-mile intervals at 3 to 5 percent faster than race pace.
3. Walk/jog 400 meters (a quarter mile) between intervals. Maintain consistent interval times and rest between intervals.
4. Cool down with an easy one-mile run.

800-METER INTERVALS

1. Stretch and warm up completely with an easy one-mile run.
2. Run six 800-meter (half-mile) intervals at 8 to 10 percent faster than race pace. Maintain consistent interval times and rest between intervals.
3. Walk/jog 200 or 400 meters (eighth to quarter mile) between intervals, depending on how hard you run the intervals.
4. Cool down with an easy one-mile run.

400-METER INTERVALS

1. Stretch and warm up completely with an easy one-mile run.
2. Run three sets of four 400-meter (quarter-mile) intervals (for a total of 12 × 400 meters) at 10 to 12 percent faster than race pace.
3. Walk/jog 200 meters (eighth mile) between intervals and rest five minutes between sets.
4. Cool down with an easy one-mile run.

NEGATIVE SPLIT INTERVALS

1. Stretch and warm up completely with an easy one-mile run. Then concentrate on running each of the following at a faster pace than the previous interval (negative splitting).
2. Run one mile at 3 to 5 percent faster than race pace.
3. Walk/jog 400-meter recovery.

4. Run 1,200 meters (three-quarters mile) at 5 to 7 percent faster than race pace.
5. Walk/jog 400-meter recovery.
6. Run 800 meters (half mile) at 8 to 10 percent faster than race pace.
7. Walk/jog 400-meter recovery.
8. Run 400 meters (quarter mile) at 10 to 12 percent faster than race pace.
9. Run an easy one-mile cooldown.

Sample Week of Speed Work

Here's a sample week to show how to incorporate endurance, strength, and speed workouts for 5K to 10K race distances:

Monday: Do a medium-distance run about 80 to 100 percent of race distance. Relax and run a smooth, controlled pace.

Tuesday: Run four 1-mile intervals. Keep interval times as consistent as possible.

Wednesday: Day off.

Thursday: Do a pyramid fartlek workout (:15 hard/:15 easy; :30 hard/:30 easy, up to 2:00 hard/2:00 easy, and back down.)

Friday: Run medium distance of 80 to 100 percent of race distance. Maintain strong pace, good form, and run tall.

Saturday: Run long, slow distance of 125 to 150 percent of race distance. Run smooth and relaxed. Enjoy the scenery along the way.

Sunday: Day off. Give your body a chance to rest and recover from the week.

Fun Ones, Bricks, and Overtraining

A great way to keep your fire lit is to mix up your workouts with plenty of variety. Try these ideas:

> **Point-to-point courses.** Instead of a loop or out-and-back course, try a point-to-point. Run from point A to point B.
> **Scenic courses.** Even if your usual training course is pretty, get some variety. Find a course that fills your soul as the miles go by.
> **Trail courses.** For an energizing lift, find a quiet trail through rolling hills or meadows to forget the straight and narrow.
> **Follow the leader.** Grab a friend or three or more and play follow-the-leader. Don't be afraid to be silly or tough.
> **Hound and hare.** With a friend or five or more, designate one as the hare and the others as the hounds. Give your hare a head start, then let the hounds loose to see who can chase down the hare.
> **Get a partner.** Training with a partner can be great therapy or just great fun. Find a partner and train together.

Bricks

Bricks are combination workouts that pair two disciplines (swim-bike or bike-run) to prepare your body for race day. Bricks are a heavy load, so they should be done well into your training season, after a solid training base in each discipline.

For most, the swim-bike transition is easier than the bike-run. So, when deciding your brick type, you'll likely want to do more bike-run bricks than swim-bike.

Set your swim-bike bricks at 30 to 50 percent of race distance and bike-run bricks at 50 to 65 percent of race distance. Remember to:

> Gradually build to these distances.
> Consider splitting your bricks early in the season by doing a swim workout in the morning and a bike in the afternoon, or bike in the morning and run in the afternoon.
> Consider a "taster" bike or run brick of 10 minutes or so to your swim or bike workout just to give your body a taste of the challenge switching from one discipline to another.
> Shorten your distances as you increase your intensity.
> Consider doing sets of shorter repeat bricks as an advanced workout and to practice your transitions.
> Listen to your body and adjust your distances as needed to avoid injury and overtraining.

Overtraining

Overtraining is the point where your training and daily stresses add up to overtax your system. A training program that may not be overtraining one week may be overtraining the next because of additional stresses at work, home, or elsewhere.

Signs of Overtraining
Be aware of overtraining signs: a high resting pulse at waking, trouble sleeping, snapping at friends or coworkers, or feeling tired all the time.

Overtraining Cure
The cure for overtraining is simple, if not wanted: Back off your training. Take a couple of days off, reduce the intensity, reduce the total amount, and get more rest. Look to cut "training fat" where you may be putting in quantity over quality.

Overtraining can lead to an injury, a cold, or just slow times, so train well, race well, have fun, and feel great!

Getting More out of Your Diary

*T*riLog is a tool that can help you get the most out of your training. As with any tool, you can get more out of it when you adjust it to fit you and your needs, that is, what's important to *you*, not the person next to you. We've provided plenty of space and flexibility in the diary pages to let you decide what and how much information to record. Whatever you record, making daily notes can be one of the best ways to keep on track to meeting your goals. Here are a couple of ways to get the most out of your diary.

Adjust to Your Needs

Adjust your notes according to your needs and training focus as you progress through your training cycles. Feel free to write inside the lines and out. In this edition, we've added a "Notes" section, which can be a great place to note how you felt, what you used for hydration or fueling, and any other comments that may be useful. Use our sections to note key training data, but, of course, be sure to make notes on *any* areas that are important to you. For example, you may focus on your diet and body weight during early stages of a training phase, while later, you may focus on total miles and heart rate training zones. Use the diary page in whatever way that works best for you.

Be Consistent

Your diary, like your training, is only as good as what you put into it. Be consistent in recording your training. Remember to note your daily and weekly miles, courses, and times. But don't forget to note how you feel during and after workouts. This subjective data can be as valuable, or more, as the objective data.

Use Tracking Charts

Use these tracking charts to see your progress.

Running Training and Race Pace Chart

This chart lets you figure (1) your pace needed to finish a given training or race distance in a projected time, (2) your total time for a given training or race distance, and (3) your quarter-mile race pace from your race finish time.

> **Race pace.** To calculate the average pace to finish in a given time: (1) find the desired finish in the appropriate distance column, then (2) find the associated pace in the pace/mile column. For example, if you want to finish a 10K in 40:23, you'd need to average 6:30 per mile. Use this per-mile pace during a race to help you judge at each mile mark whether or not you're on pace for your goal finish time.

> **Finish time.** To calculate your total time for a given training or race distance based on a per-mile average, (1) find the pace per mile in the pace/mile column, and (2) find the associated total time in the distance column. Use this total time to see if you're running your endurance runs at the right pace or to estimate your finish time for a training or race distance.

> **Quarter-mile pace.** To find your quarter-mile interval race pace (1) locate your race finish time in the appropriate distance column and (2) find the associated quarter-mile pace in the pace-per-quarter-mile column. Use this quarter-mile pace with the Running Interval Training Pace Chart to plan your interval training.

Running Interval Training Pace Chart

This chart will help you set your goal speed-training intervals.

To find your goal speed-training intervals, (1) find your quarter-mile race pace on the Running Training and Race Pace Chart, (2) find your quarter-mile race pace in the pace-per-quarter-mile column in this chart, (3) use the associated interval times from the appropriate eighth-mile, quarter-mile, half-mile, or one-mile columns. Each interval distance shows a range of interval goal times to target as you work to build your speed. Use these and the tips in "Running Speed Work" as guidelines for your intervals; adjust your interval times to your conditioning as it changes throughout your training season.

Map to Race Day Worksheet

This worksheet will help you plan a multiweek training program for a specific event.

To plan your training, (1) mark week 1, 2, 3, or 4 as your training peak, depending on the distance of your event. (The longer the event, say Ironman or 70.3 [Half Ironman], the more you may want two, three, or four weeks of taper prior to race day. The shorter the race, the shorter your taper will likely be, say one or two weeks prior to an Olympic or sprint distance race.) (2) Mark the week number that you will begin your training. (3) Plan each week's training in a schedule that will allow you to build gradually from your training start point to your training peak (and prerace taper). Never increase mileage more than 10 percent per week, and allow time to stay at training plateaus before moving on to subsequent levels of training.

Race Results Summary

The Race Results Summary lets you note in one place your entire race results. Remember to note any comments about the race or conditions that affected your results and review this page against your training to see what works best for you.

Cumulative Mileage Chart

The Cumulative Mileage Chart lets you graph your weekly training mileage. There is a vertical column for each week. Note the week date along the bottom of the chart and graph your weekly mileage to the corresponding distance level. Throughout your training season, review your cumulative mileage chart to note how your total training volume affects your race results, racing fitness, and any of your other goals or issues.

Running Training and Race Pace Chart

Pace per Mile	Pace per ¼ Mile	5K	8K*	10K	15K	10 Miles	13.1 Miles	25K	26.2 Miles
4:30	1:07	13:59	22:22	27:58	41:57	45:00	58:57	1:09:54	1:57:54
4:40	1:10	14:30	23:12	29:00	43:30	46:40	1:01:08	1:12:30	2:02:16
4:50	1:12	15:01	24:02	30:02	45:03	48:20	1:03:19	1:15:05	2:06:38
5:00	1:15	15:32	24:51	31:04	46:36	50:00	1:05:30	1:17:40	2:11:00
5:10	1:18	16:03	25:41	32:06	48:09	51:40	1:07:41	1:20:16	2:15:22
5:20	1:20	16:34	26:31	33:08	49:43	53:20	1:09:52	1:22:51	2:19:44
5:30	1:23	17:05	27:20	34:11	51:16	55:00	1:12:03	1:25:26	2:24:06
5:40	1:25	17:36	28:10	35:13	52:49	56:40	1:14:14	1:28:02	2:28:28
5:50	1:27	18:07	29:00	36:15	54:22	58:20	1:16:25	1:30:37	2:32:50
6:00	1:30	18:38	29:50	37:17	55:55	1:00:00	1:18:36	1:33:12	2:37:12
6:10	1:33	19:10	30:39	38:19	57:29	1:01:40	1:20:47	1:35:48	2:41:34
6:20	1:35	19:41	31:29	39:21	59:02	1:03:20	1:22:58	1:38:23	2:45:56
6:30	1:38	20:12	32:19	40:23	1:00:35	1:05:00	1:25:09	1:40:58	2:50:18
6:40	1:40	20:43	33:08	41:25	1:02:08	1:06:40	1:27:20	1:43:34	2:54:40
6:50	1:42	21:14	33:58	42:28	1:03:41	1:08:20	1:29:31	1:46:09	2:59:02
7:00	1:45	21:45	34:48	43:30	1:05:15	1:10:00	1:31:42	1:48:44	3:03:24
7:10	1:47	22:16	35:38	44:32	1:06:48	1:11:40	1:33:53	1:51:20	3:07:46
7:20	1:50	22:47	36:27	45:34	1:08:21	1:13:20	1:36:04	1:53:55	3:12:08
7:30	1:52	23:18	37:17	46:36	1:09:54	1:15:00	1:38:15	1:56:30	3:16:30
7:40	1:55	23:49	38:07	47:38	1:11:27	1:16:40	1:40:26	1:59:06	3:20:52
7:50	1:58	24:20	38:56	48:40	1:13:01	1:18:20	1:42:37	2:01:41	3:25:14
8:00	2:00	24:51	39:46	49:43	1:14:34	1:20:00	1:44:48	2:04:16	3:29:36
8:10	2:02	25:22	40:36	50:45	1:16:07	1:21:40	1:46:59	2:06:52	3:33:58
8:20	2:05	25:53	41:25	51:47	1:17:40	1:23:20	1:49:10	2:09:27	3:38:20
8:30	2:07	26:24	42:15	52:49	1:19:13	1:25:00	1:51:21	2:12:02	3:42:42
8:40	2:10	26:56	43:05	53:51	1:20:47	1:26:40	1:53:32	2:14:38	3:47:04
8:50	2:13	27:27	43:55	54:53	1:22:20	1:28:20	1:55:43	2:17:13	3:51:26
9:00	2:15	27:58	44:44	55:55	1:23:53	1:30:00	1:57:54	2:19:49	3:55:48
9:10	2:17	28:29	45:34	56:58	1:25:26	1:31:40	2:00:05	2:22:24	4:00:10
9:20	2:20	29:00	46:24	58:00	1:27:00	1:33:20	2:02:16	2:24:59	4:04:32
9:30	2:23	29:31	47:13	59:02	1:28:33	1:35:00	2:04:27	2:27:35	4:08:54
9:40	2:25	30:02	48:03	1:00:04	1:30:06	1:36:40	2:06:38	2:30:10	4:13:16
9:50	2:28	30:33	48:53	1:01:06	1:31:39	1:38:20	2:08:49	2:32:45	4:17:38
10:00	2:30	31:04	49:43	1:02:08	1:33:12	1:40:00	2:11:00	2:35:21	4:22:00
11:00	2:45	34:11	54:41	1:08:21	1:42:32	1:50:00	2:24:06	2:50:53	4:48:12
12:00	3:00	37:17	59:39	1:14:34	1:51:51	2:00:00	2:37:12	3:06:25	5:14:24
13:00	3:15	40:23	1:04:37	1:20:47	2:01:10	2:10:00	2:50:18	3:21:57	5:40:36
14:00	3:30	43:30	1:09:36	1:27:00	2:10:29	2:20:00	3:03:24	3:37:29	6:06:48
15:00	3:45	46:36	1:14:34	1:33:12	2:19:49	2:30:00	3:16:30	3:53:01	6:33:00
16:00	4:00	49:43	1:19:32	1:39:25	2:29:08	2:40:00	3:29:36	4:08:33	6:59:12
17:00	4:15	52:49	1:24:30	1:45:38	2:38:27	2:50:00	3:42:42	4:24:05	7:25:24
18:00	4:30	55:55	1:29:29	1:51:51	2:47:46	3:00:00	3:55:48	4:39:37	7:51:36
19:00	4:45	59:02	1:34:27	1:58:04	2:57:05	3:10:00	4:08:54	4:55:09	8:17:48
20:00	5:00	1:02:08	1:39:25	2:04:16	3:06:25	3:20:00	4:22:00	5:10:41	8:44:00

*Use 8K distance as an equivalent to 5 miles since 8K equals 4.97 miles.

Running Interval Training Pace Chart

RACE PACE	TRAINING PACE FOR INTERVALS (AS % OF RACE PACE)			
per ¼ Mile	⅛ Mile (200 Meters) 112%–115%	¼ Mile (400 Meters) 110%–112%	½ Mile (800 Meters) 108%–110%	1 Mile (1,600 Meters) 103%–105%
1:08	:29–:30	:59–1:01	2:02–2:04	4:17–4:22
1:10	:30–:31	1:02–1:03	2:06–2:09	4:26–4:32
1:12	:31–:32	1:04–1:05	2:10–2:13	4:35–4:41
1:15	:32–:33	1:06–1:08	2:15–2:18	4:45–4:51
1:17	:33–:34	1:08–1:10	2:19–2:23	4:54–5:01
1:20	:34–:35	1:10–1:12	2:24–2:27	5:04–5:10
1:22	:35–:36	1:13–1:14	2:28–2:32	5:13–5:20
1:25	:36–:37	1:15–1:17	2:33–2:36	5:23–5:30
1:28	:37–:39	1:17–1:19	2:38–2:41	5:33–5:40
1:30	:38–:40	1:19–1:21	2:42–2:46	5:42–5:49
1:33	:39–:41	1:21–1:23	2:47–2:50	5:52–5:59
1:35	:40–:42	1:24–1:26	2:51–2:55	6:01–6:09
1:37	:41–:43	1:26–1:28	2:55–2:59	6:10–6:18
1:40	:42–:44	1:28–1:30	3:00–3:04	6:20–6:28
1:43	:44–:45	1:30–1:32	3:05–3:09	6:30–6:38
1:45	:45–:46	1:32–1:35	3:09–3:13	6:39–6:47
1:48	:46–:47	1:35–1:37	3:14–3:18	6:49–6:57
1:50	:47–:48	1:37–1:39	3:18–3:22	6:58–7:07
1:52	:48–:49	1:39–1:41	3:22–3:27	7:07–7:16
1:55	:49–:51	1:41–1:44	3:27–3:32	7:17–7:26
1:57	:50–:52	1:43–1:46	3:31–3:36	7:26–7:36
2:00	:51–:53	1:46–1:48	3:36–3:41	7:36–7:46
2:03	:52–:54	1:48–1:50	3:41–3:45	7:46–7:55
2:05	:53–:55	1:50–1:53	3:45–3:50	7:55–8:05
2:07	:54–:56	1:52–1:55	3:49–3:55	8:04–8:15
2:10	:55–:57	1:54–1:57	3:54–3:59	8:14–8:24
2:12	:56–:58	1:57–1:59	3:58–4:04	8:23–8:34
2:15	:57–:59	1:59–2:02	4:03–4:08	8:33–8:44
2:18	:58–1:01	2:01–2:04	4:08–4:13	8:43–8:54
2:20	1:00–1:02	2:03–2:06	4:12–4:18	8:52–9:03
2:23	1:01–1:03	2:05–2:08	4:17–4:22	9:02–9:13
2:25	1:02–1:04	2:08–2:11	4:21–4:27	9:11–9:23
2:27	1:03–1:05	2:10–2:13	4:25–4:31	9:20–9:32
2:30	1:04–1:06	2:12–2:15	4:30–4:36	9:30–9:42
2:45	1:10–1:13	2:25–2:29	4:57–5:04	10:27–10:40
3:00	1:16–1:19	2:38–2:42	5:24–5:31	11:24–11:38
3:15	1:23–1:26	2:52–2:56	5:51–5:59	12:21–12:37
3:30	1:29–1:32	3:05–3:09	6:18–6:26	13:18–13:35
3:45	1:36–1:39	3:18–3:23	6:45–6:54	14:15–14:33
4:00	1:42–1:46	3:31–3:36	7:12–7:22	15:12–15:31
4:15	1:48–1:52	3:44–3:50	7:39–7:49	16:09–16:29
4:30	1:55–1:59	3:58–4:03	8:06–8:17	17:06–17:28
4:45	2:01–2:05	4:11–4:17	8:33–8:44	18:03–18:26
5:00	2:07–2:12	4:24–4:30	9:00–9:12	19:00–19:24

Map to Race Day Worksheet

	Monday	Tuesday	Wednesday	Thursday	Friday	Saturday	Sunday	Weekly Total
WEEK 13	Swim:____ Bike:____ Run:____	Swim:____ Bike:____ Run:____	Swim:____ Bike:____ Run:____	Swim:____ Bike:____ Run:____	Swim:____ Bike:____ Run:____	Swim:____ Bike:____ Run:____	Swim:____ Bike:____ Run:____	☐ ☐ ☐
WEEK 12	Swim:____ Bike:____ Run:____	Swim:____ Bike:____ Run:____	Swim:____ Bike:____ Run:____	Swim:____ Bike:____ Run:____	Swim:____ Bike:____ Run:____	Swim:____ Bike:____ Run:____	Swim:____ Bike:____ Run:____	☐ ☐ ☐
WEEK 11	Swim:____ Bike:____ Run:____	Swim:____ Bike:____ Run:____	Swim:____ Bike:____ Run:____	Swim:____ Bike:____ Run:____	Swim:____ Bike:____ Run:____	Swim:____ Bike:____ Run:____	Swim:____ Bike:____ Run:____	☐ ☐ ☐
WEEK 10	Swim:____ Bike:____ Run:____	Swim:____ Bike:____ Run:____	Swim:____ Bike:____ Run:____	Swim:____ Bike:____ Run:____	Swim:____ Bike:____ Run:____	Swim:____ Bike:____ Run:____	Swim:____ Bike:____ Run:____	☐ ☐ ☐
WEEK 9	Swim:____ Bike:____ Run:____	Swim:____ Bike:____ Run:____	Swim:____ Bike:____ Run:____	Swim:____ Bike:____ Run:____	Swim:____ Bike:____ Run:____	Swim:____ Bike:____ Run:____	Swim:____ Bike:____ Run:____	☐ ☐ ☐
WEEK 8	Swim:____ Bike:____ Run:____	Swim:____ Bike:____ Run:____	Swim:____ Bike:____ Run:____	Swim:____ Bike:____ Run:____	Swim:____ Bike:____ Run:____	Swim:____ Bike:____ Run:____	Swim:____ Bike:____ Run:____	☐ ☐ ☐
WEEK 7	Swim:____ Bike:____ Run:____	Swim:____ Bike:____ Run:____	Swim:____ Bike:____ Run:____	Swim:____ Bike:____ Run:____	Swim:____ Bike:____ Run:____	Swim:____ Bike:____ Run:____	Swim:____ Bike:____ Run:____	☐ ☐ ☐

Map to Race Day Worksheet

	Monday	Tuesday	Wednesday	Thursday	Friday	Saturday	Sunday	Weekly Total
WEEK 6	Swim:____ Bike:____ Run:____	Swim:____ Bike:____ Run:____	Swim:____ Bike:____ Run:____	Swim:____ Bike:____ Run:____	Swim:____ Bike:____ Run:____	Swim:____ Bike:____ Run:____	Swim:____ Bike:____ Run:____	
WEEK 5	Swim:____ Bike:____ Run:____	Swim:____ Bike:____ Run:____	Swim:____ Bike:____ Run:____	Swim:____ Bike:____ Run:____	Swim:____ Bike:____ Run:____	Swim:____ Bike:____ Run:____	Swim:____ Bike:____ Run:____	
WEEK 4	Swim:____ Bike:____ Run:____	Swim:____ Bike:____ Run:____	Swim:____ Bike:____ Run:____	Swim:____ Bike:____ Run:____	Swim:____ Bike:____ Run:____	Swim:____ Bike:____ Run:____	Swim:____ Bike:____ Run:____	
WEEK 3	Swim:____ Bike:____ Run:____	Swim:____ Bike:____ Run:____	Swim:____ Bike:____ Run:____	Swim:____ Bike:____ Run:____	Swim:____ Bike:____ Run:____	Swim:____ Bike:____ Run:____	Swim:____ Bike:____ Run:____	
WEEK 2	Swim:____ Bike:____ Run:____	Swim:____ Bike:____ Run:____	Swim:____ Bike:____ Run:____	Swim:____ Bike:____ Run:____	Swim:____ Bike:____ Run:____	Swim:____ Bike:____ Run:____	Swim:____ Bike:____ Run:____	
WEEK 1	Swim:____ Bike:____ Run:____	Swim:____ Bike:____ Run:____	Swim:____ Bike:____ Run:____	Swim:____ Bike:____ Run:____	Swim:____ Bike:____ Run:____	Swim:____ Bike:____ Run:____	Swim:____ Bike:____ Run:____	
WEEK 0/RACE WEEK	Swim:____ Bike:____ Run:____	Swim:____ Bike:____ Run:____	Swim:____ Bike:____ Run:____	Swim:____ Bike:____ Run:____	Swim:____ Bike:____ Run:____	Swim:____ Bike:____ Run:____	Swim:____ Bike:____ Run:____	

Race Results Summary

Race Name, Date, Distances: *Sample Entry*

Comments/Notes:

FINISH PLACE			TIME												
Division	Overall	Sex	Finish	SWIM	Pace	Place	T1	BIKE	Pace	Place	T2	RUN	Pace	Place
95	1,014	762	3:16:51	30:54	9:46 min/K	70	9:46	1:10	15.4 mph	977	12:52	1:12	10:12 min/mile	951

Race Name, Date, Distances:

Comments/Notes:

FINISH PLACE			TIME												
Division	Overall	Sex	Finish	SWIM	Pace	Place	T1	BIKE	Pace	Place	T2	RUN	Pace	Place

Race Name, Date, Distances:

Comments/Notes:

FINISH PLACE			TIME												
Division	Overall	Sex	Finish	SWIM	Pace	Place	T1	BIKE	Pace	Place	T2	RUN	Pace	Place

Race Results Summary

Race Name, Date, Distances: _____

Comments/Notes: _____

FINISH PLACE			TIME	SWIM			T1	BIKE			T2	RUN		
Division	Overall	Sex	Finish		Pace	Place			Pace	Place			Pace	Place

Race Name, Date, Distances: _____

Comments/Notes: _____

FINISH PLACE			TIME	SWIM			T1	BIKE			T2	RUN		
Division	Overall	Sex	Finish		Pace	Place			Pace	Place			Pace	Place

Race Name, Date, Distances: _____

Comments/Notes: _____

FINISH PLACE			TIME	SWIM			T1	BIKE			T2	RUN		
Division	Overall	Sex	Finish		Pace	Place			Pace	Place			Pace	Place

Cumulative Mileage Chart

Swim: ▲; Bike: ●; Run: ✖

Note: Yards ÷ 1,760 = miles

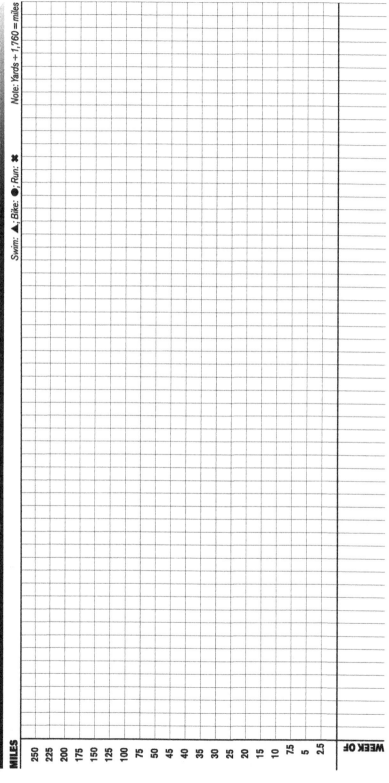

MILES

250
225
200
175
150
125
100
75
50
45
40
35
30
25
20
15
10
7.5
5
2.5

WEEK OF

PART 2
Training Diary

Sample Diary Page

Monday
Date 5/27

Swim 500 warm-up; 50 kick; 5 x 200 @ 3:15 (3:01, 3:02, 3:02, 3:05, 3:04); 100 kick; 5 x 100 @ 1:45
(1:31, 1:32, 1:35, 1:37, 1:35); 50 cooldown; felt smooth and strong. Yards 2,200

Bike Tiburon Loop: Mill Valley, Tiburon, loop, and home; legs felt sluggish on hills; need a day off!
Miles/Time 42/2:41

Run Ferry Building: Marina Green to ballpark to Ferry building; felt fresh and fast after
day off Miles/Time 5.5 mi/42:33

Notes Fueling and hydration worked well on bike and run!

Starting line, L.A. Triathlon

"The secret of getting ahead is getting started."

–Sally Berger

WEEK 1

Monday

Date _____

Swim _____
_____ Yards _____
Bike _____
_____ Miles/Time _____
Run _____
_____ Miles/Time _____
Notes _____

Tuesday

Date _____

Swim _____
_____ Yards _____
Bike _____
_____ Miles/Time _____
Run _____
_____ Miles/Time _____
Notes _____

Wednesday

Date _____

Swim _____
_____ Yards _____
Bike _____
_____ Miles/Time _____
Run _____
_____ Miles/Time _____
Notes _____

Thursday

Date _____

Swim _____
_____ Yards _____
Bike _____
_____ Miles/Time _____
Run _____
_____ Miles/Time _____
Notes _____

Friday   Date

Swim _____

_____ Yards _____

Bike _____

_____ Miles/Time _____

Run _____

_____ Miles/Time _____

Notes _____

Saturday   Date

Swim _____

_____ Yards _____

Bike _____

_____ Miles/Time _____

Run _____

_____ Miles/Time _____

Notes _____

Sunday   Date

Swim _____

_____ Yards _____

Bike _____

_____ Miles/Time _____

Run _____

_____ Miles/Time _____

Notes _____

Review

Goals/Notes _____

_____

_____

_____

_____

Swim Total [   ]   **Bike Total** [   ]   **Run Total** [   ]

WEEK 2

Monday
Date _____

Swim _____
_____ Yards _____
Bike _____
_____ Miles/Time _____
Run _____
_____ Miles/Time _____
Notes _____

Tuesday
Date _____

Swim _____
_____ Yards _____
Bike _____
_____ Miles/Time _____
Run _____
_____ Miles/Time _____
Notes _____

Wednesday
Date _____

Swim _____
_____ Yards _____
Bike _____
_____ Miles/Time _____
Run _____
_____ Miles/Time _____
Notes _____

Thursday
Date _____

Swim _____
_____ Yards _____
Bike _____
_____ Miles/Time _____
Run _____
_____ Miles/Time _____
Notes _____

Friday   Date

Swim _____
_____ Yards _____

Bike _____
_____ Miles/Time _____

Run _____
_____ Miles/Time _____

Notes _____

Saturday   Date

Swim _____
_____ Yards _____

Bike _____
_____ Miles/Time _____

Run _____
_____ Miles/Time _____

Notes _____

Sunday   Date

Swim _____
_____ Yards _____

Bike _____
_____ Miles/Time _____

Run _____
_____ Miles/Time _____

Notes _____

Review

Goals/Notes _____
_____
_____
_____
_____

Swim Total [ ]   **Bike Total** [ ]   **Run Total** [ ]

Monday

Date _____

Swim _____

_____ Yards _____

Bike _____

_____ Miles/Time _____

Run _____

_____ Miles/Time _____

Notes _____

Tuesday

Date _____

Swim _____

_____ Yards _____

Bike _____

_____ Miles/Time _____

Run _____

_____ Miles/Time _____

Notes _____

Wednesday

Date _____

Swim _____

_____ Yards _____

Bike _____

_____ Miles/Time _____

Run _____

_____ Miles/Time _____

Notes _____

Thursday

Date _____

Swim _____

_____ Yards _____

Bike _____

_____ Miles/Time _____

Run _____

_____ Miles/Time _____

Notes _____

Friday   Date

Swim _____
_____ Yards _____

Bike _____
_____ Miles/Time _____

Run _____
_____ Miles/Time _____

Notes _____

Saturday   Date

Swim _____
_____ Yards _____

Bike _____
_____ Miles/Time _____

Run _____
_____ Miles/Time _____

Notes _____

Sunday   Date

Swim _____
_____ Yards _____

Bike _____
_____ Miles/Time _____

Run _____
_____ Miles/Time _____

Notes _____

Review

Goals/Notes _____
_____
_____
_____
_____

Swim Total		**Bike Total**		**Run Total**	

Monday
Date _____

Swim _____
_____ Yards _____

Bike _____
_____ Miles/Time _____

Run _____
_____ Miles/Time _____

Notes _____

Tuesday
Date _____

Swim _____
_____ Yards _____

Bike _____
_____ Miles/Time _____

Run _____
_____ Miles/Time _____

Notes _____

Wednesday
Date _____

Swim _____
_____ Yards _____

Bike _____
_____ Miles/Time _____

Run _____
_____ Miles/Time _____

Notes _____

Thursday
Date _____

Swim _____
_____ Yards _____

Bike _____
_____ Miles/Time _____

Run _____
_____ Miles/Time _____

Notes _____

Friday

Date

Swim _____
_____ Yards _____

Bike _____
_____ Miles/Time _____

Run _____
_____ Miles/Time _____

Notes _____

Saturday

Date

Swim _____
_____ Yards _____

Bike _____
_____ Miles/Time _____

Run _____
_____ Miles/Time _____

Notes _____

Sunday

Date

Swim _____
_____ Yards _____

Bike _____
_____ Miles/Time _____

Run _____
_____ Miles/Time _____

Notes _____

Review

Goals/Notes _____
_____
_____
_____
_____

Swim Total [　　　] **Bike Total** [　　　] **Run Total** [　　　]

WEEK 5

Monday   Date

Swim _____

_____ Yards _____

Bike _____

_____ Miles/Time _____

Run _____

_____ Miles/Time _____

Notes _____

Tuesday   Date

Swim _____

_____ Yards _____

Bike _____

_____ Miles/Time _____

Run _____

_____ Miles/Time _____

Notes _____

Wednesday   Date

Swim _____

_____ Yards _____

Bike _____

_____ Miles/Time _____

Run _____

_____ Miles/Time _____

Notes _____

Thursday   Date

Swim _____

_____ Yards _____

Bike _____

_____ Miles/Time _____

Run _____

_____ Miles/Time _____

Notes _____

Friday _____ Date _____

Swim _____
_____ Yards _____

Bike _____
_____ Miles/Time _____

Run _____
_____ Miles/Time _____

Notes _____

Saturday _____ Date _____

Swim _____
_____ Yards _____

Bike _____
_____ Miles/Time _____

Run _____
_____ Miles/Time _____

Notes _____

Sunday _____ Date _____

Swim _____
_____ Yards _____

Bike _____
_____ Miles/Time _____

Run _____
_____ Miles/Time _____

Notes _____

Review

Goals/Notes _____
_____
_____
_____
_____

Swim Total [   ]   **Bike Total** [   ]   **Run Total** [   ]

Monday _____ Date _____

Swim _____

_____ Yards _____

Bike _____

_____ Miles/Time ____

Run _____

_____ Miles/Time ____

Notes _____

Tuesday _____ Date _____

Swim _____

_____ Yards _____

Bike _____

_____ Miles/Time ____

Run _____

_____ Miles/Time ____

Notes _____

Wednesday _____ Date _____

Swim _____

_____ Yards _____

Bike _____

_____ Miles/Time ____

Run _____

_____ Miles/Time ____

Notes _____

Thursday _____ Date _____

Swim _____

_____ Yards _____

Bike _____

_____ Miles/Time ____

Run _____

_____ Miles/Time ____

Notes _____

6

Friday
Date _____

Swim _____
_____ Yards _____

Bike _____
_____ Miles/Time _____

Run _____
_____ Miles/Time _____

Notes _____

Saturday
Date _____

Swim _____
_____ Yards _____

Bike _____
_____ Miles/Time _____

Run _____
_____ Miles/Time _____

Notes _____

Sunday
Date _____

Swim _____
_____ Yards _____

Bike _____
_____ Miles/Time _____

Run _____
_____ Miles/Time _____

Notes _____

Review

Goals/Notes _____
_____
_____
_____
_____

Swim Total [ ]   **Bike Total** [ ]   **Run Total** [ ]

Monday _____ Date _____

Swim _____

_____ Yards _____

Bike _____

_____ Miles/Time _____

Run _____

_____ Miles/Time _____

Notes _____

Tuesday _____ Date _____

Swim _____

_____ Yards _____

Bike _____

_____ Miles/Time _____

Run _____

_____ Miles/Time _____

Notes _____

Wednesday _____ Date _____

Swim _____

_____ Yards _____

Bike _____

_____ Miles/Time _____

Run _____

_____ Miles/Time _____

Notes _____

Thursday _____ Date _____

Swim _____

_____ Yards _____

Bike _____

_____ Miles/Time _____

Run _____

_____ Miles/Time _____

Notes _____

Friday

Date _____

Swim _____

_____ Yards _____

Bike _____

_____ Miles/Time _____

Run _____

_____ Miles/Time _____

Notes _____

Saturday

Date _____

Swim _____

_____ Yards _____

Bike _____

_____ Miles/Time _____

Run _____

_____ Miles/Time _____

Notes _____

Sunday

Date _____

Swim _____

_____ Yards _____

Bike _____

_____ Miles/Time _____

Run _____

_____ Miles/Time _____

Notes _____

Review

Goals/Notes _____

_____

_____

_____

_____

Swim Total [____] **Bike Total** [____] **Run Total** [____]

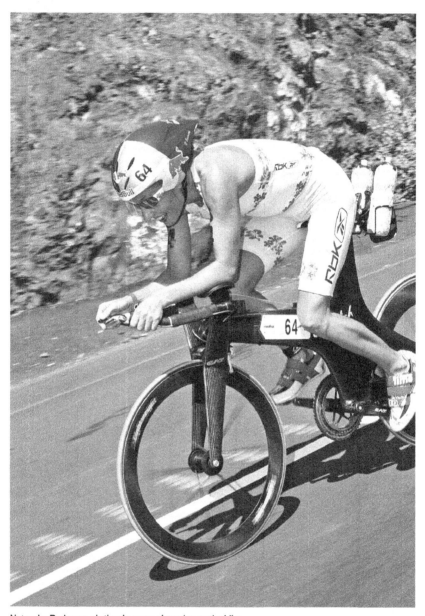

Natascha Badmann, six-time Ironman champion on the bike

*"People begin to become successful
the minute they decide to be."*

—Harvey Mackay

On the run, Maui Xterra World Championship

*"It is better to wear out one's shoes
than one's sheets."*

—Genoese proverb

Monday   Date

Swim _____

_____ Yards _____

Bike _____

_____ Miles/Time _____

Run _____

_____ Miles/Time _____

Notes _____

Tuesday   Date

Swim _____

_____ Yards _____

Bike _____

_____ Miles/Time _____

Run _____

_____ Miles/Time _____

Notes _____

Wednesday   Date

Swim _____

_____ Yards _____

Bike _____

_____ Miles/Time _____

Run _____

_____ Miles/Time _____

Notes _____

Thursday   Date

Swim _____

_____ Yards _____

Bike _____

_____ Miles/Time _____

Run _____

_____ Miles/Time _____

Notes _____

Friday

Date _____

Swim _____

_____ Yards _____

Bike _____

_____ Miles/Time _____

Run _____

_____ Miles/Time _____

Notes _____

Saturday

Date _____

Swim _____

_____ Yards _____

Bike _____

_____ Miles/Time _____

Run _____

_____ Miles/Time _____

Notes _____

Sunday

Date _____

Swim _____

_____ Yards _____

Bike _____

_____ Miles/Time _____

Run _____

_____ Miles/Time _____

Notes _____

Review

Goals/Notes _____

_____

_____

_____

_____

Swim Total [   ] **Bike Total** [   ] **Run Total** [   ]

Monday   **Date**

Swim _____

_____ Yards _____

Bike _____

_____ Miles/Time _____

Run _____

_____ Miles/Time _____

Notes _____

Tuesday   **Date**

Swim _____

_____ Yards _____

Bike _____

_____ Miles/Time _____

Run _____

_____ Miles/Time _____

Notes _____

Wednesday   **Date**

Swim _____

_____ Yards _____

Bike _____

_____ Miles/Time _____

Run _____

_____ Miles/Time _____

Notes _____

Thursday   **Date**

Swim _____

_____ Yards _____

Bike _____

_____ Miles/Time _____

Run _____

_____ Miles/Time _____

Notes _____

Friday

Date _____

Swim _____
_____ Yards _____

Bike _____
_____ Miles/Time _____

Run _____
_____ Miles/Time _____

Notes _____

Saturday

Date _____

Swim _____
_____ Yards _____

Bike _____
_____ Miles/Time _____

Run _____
_____ Miles/Time _____

Notes _____

Sunday

Date _____

Swim _____
_____ Yards _____

Bike _____
_____ Miles/Time _____

Run _____
_____ Miles/Time _____

Notes _____

Review

Goals/Notes _____
_____
_____
_____

Swim Total [____]   **Bike Total** [____]   **Run Total** [____]

WEEK 10

Monday
Date _____

Swim _____
_____ Yards _____
Bike _____
_____ Miles/Time _____
Run _____
_____ Miles/Time _____
Notes _____

Tuesday
Date _____

Swim _____
_____ Yards _____
Bike _____
_____ Miles/Time _____
Run _____
_____ Miles/Time _____
Notes _____

Wednesday
Date _____

Swim _____
_____ Yards _____
Bike _____
_____ Miles/Time _____
Run _____
_____ Miles/Time _____
Notes _____

Thursday
Date _____

Swim _____
_____ Yards _____
Bike _____
_____ Miles/Time _____
Run _____
_____ Miles/Time _____
Notes _____

WEEK 10

Friday
Date _____

Swim _____
_____ Yards _____

Bike _____
_____ Miles/Time _____

Run _____
_____ Miles/Time _____

Notes _____

Saturday
Date _____

Swim _____
_____ Yards _____

Bike _____
_____ Miles/Time _____

Run _____
_____ Miles/Time _____

Notes _____

Sunday
Date _____

Swim _____
_____ Yards _____

Bike _____
_____ Miles/Time _____

Run _____
_____ Miles/Time _____

Notes _____

Review

Goals/Notes _____
_____
_____
_____
_____

Swim Total [____]   **Bike Total** [____]   **Run Total** [____]

WEEK 11

Monday
Date _____

Swim _____
_____ Yards _____
Bike _____
_____ Miles/Time _____
Run _____
_____ Miles/Time _____
Notes _____

Tuesday
Date _____

Swim _____
_____ Yards _____
Bike _____
_____ Miles/Time _____
Run _____
_____ Miles/Time _____
Notes _____

Wednesday
Date _____

Swim _____
_____ Yards _____
Bike _____
_____ Miles/Time _____
Run _____
_____ Miles/Time _____
Notes _____

Thursday
Date _____

Swim _____
_____ Yards _____
Bike _____
_____ Miles/Time _____
Run _____
_____ Miles/Time _____
Notes _____

Friday   Date

Swim _____
_____ Yards _____

Bike _____
_____ Miles/Time _____

Run _____
_____ Miles/Time _____

Notes _____

Saturday   Date

Swim _____
_____ Yards _____

Bike _____
_____ Miles/Time _____

Run _____
_____ Miles/Time _____

Notes _____

Sunday   Date

Swim _____
_____ Yards _____

Bike _____
_____ Miles/Time _____

Run _____
_____ Miles/Time _____

Notes _____

Review

Goals/Notes _____
_____
_____
_____
_____

| **Swim Total** | | **Bike Total** | | **Run Total** | |

WEEK 12

Monday
Date

Swim _____
_____ Yards _____

Bike _____
_____ Miles/Time _____

Run _____
_____ Miles/Time _____

Notes _____

Tuesday
Date

Swim _____
_____ Yards _____

Bike _____
_____ Miles/Time _____

Run _____
_____ Miles/Time _____

Notes _____

Wednesday
Date

Swim _____
_____ Yards _____

Bike _____
_____ Miles/Time _____

Run _____
_____ Miles/Time _____

Notes _____

Thursday
Date

Swim _____
_____ Yards _____

Bike _____
_____ Miles/Time _____

Run _____
_____ Miles/Time _____

Notes _____

Friday

Date

Swim _____

_____ Yards _____

Bike _____

_____ Miles/Time _____

Run _____

_____ Miles/Time _____

Notes _____

Saturday

Date

Swim _____

_____ Yards _____

Bike _____

_____ Miles/Time _____

Run _____

_____ Miles/Time _____

Notes _____

Sunday

Date

Swim _____

_____ Yards _____

Bike _____

_____ Miles/Time _____

Run _____

_____ Miles/Time _____

Notes _____

Review

Goals/Notes _____

_____

_____

_____

_____

Swim Total	Bike Total	Run Total

Monday

Date _____

Swim _____

_____ Yards _____

Bike _____

_____ Miles/Time _____

Run _____

_____ Miles/Time _____

Notes _____

Tuesday

Date _____

Swim _____

_____ Yards _____

Bike _____

_____ Miles/Time _____

Run _____

_____ Miles/Time _____

Notes _____

Wednesday

Date _____

Swim _____

_____ Yards _____

Bike _____

_____ Miles/Time _____

Run _____

_____ Miles/Time _____

Notes _____

Thursday

Date _____

Swim _____

_____ Yards _____

Bike _____

_____ Miles/Time _____

Run _____

_____ Miles/Time _____

Notes _____

Friday
Date

Swim

Yards

Bike

Miles/Time

Run

Miles/Time

Notes

Saturday
Date

Swim

Yards

Bike

Miles/Time

Run

Miles/Time

Notes

Sunday
Date

Swim

Yards

Bike

Miles/Time

Run

Miles/Time

Notes

Review

Goals/Notes

Swim Total

Bike Total

Run Total

Monday   Date

Swim _____

_____ Yards _____

Bike _____

_____ Miles/Time _____

Run _____

_____ Miles/Time _____

Notes _____

Tuesday   Date

Swim _____

_____ Yards _____

Bike _____

_____ Miles/Time _____

Run _____

_____ Miles/Time _____

Notes _____

Wednesday   Date

Swim _____

_____ Yards _____

Bike _____

_____ Miles/Time _____

Run _____

_____ Miles/Time _____

Notes _____

Thursday   Date

Swim _____

_____ Yards _____

Bike _____

_____ Miles/Time _____

Run _____

_____ Miles/Time _____

Notes _____

Friday

Date _____

Swim _____

_____ Yards _____

Bike _____

_____ Miles/Time _____

Run _____

_____ Miles/Time _____

Notes _____

Saturday

Date _____

Swim _____

_____ Yards _____

Bike _____

_____ Miles/Time _____

Run _____

_____ Miles/Time _____

Notes _____

Sunday

Date _____

Swim _____

_____ Yards _____

Bike _____

_____ Miles/Time _____

Run _____

_____ Miles/Time _____

Notes _____

Review

Goals/Notes _____

_____

_____

_____

_____

Swim Total [   ]   **Bike Total** [   ]   **Run Total** [   ]

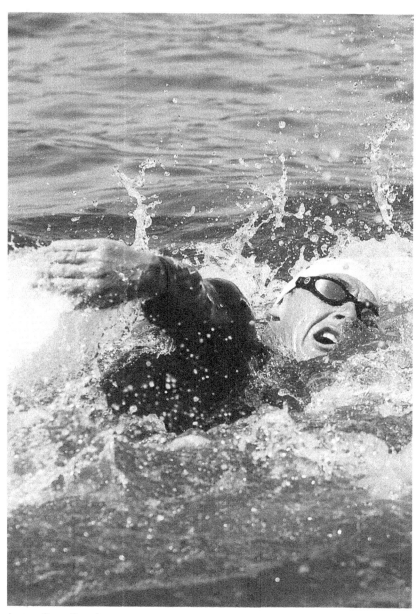

A competitor on the swim

"First say to yourself what you would be;
and then do what you have to do."

—Epictetus

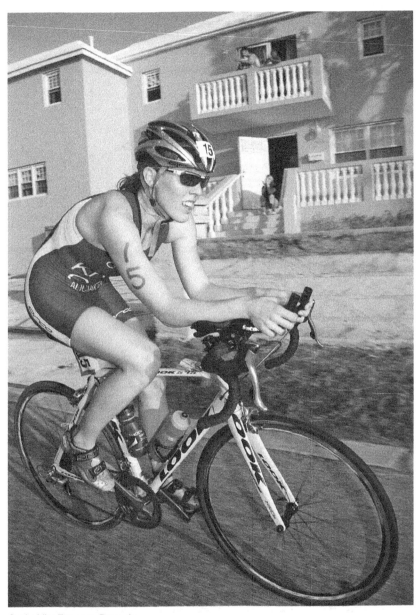
On the bike, Escape to Bermuda

"Life is either a daring adventure or nothing."
–Helen Keller

WEEK 15

Monday   Date

Swim _____

_____ Yards _____

Bike _____

_____ Miles/Time _____

Run _____

_____ Miles/Time _____

Notes _____

Tuesday   Date

Swim _____

_____ Yards _____

Bike _____

_____ Miles/Time _____

Run _____

_____ Miles/Time _____

Notes _____

Wednesday   Date

Swim _____

_____ Yards _____

Bike _____

_____ Miles/Time _____

Run _____

_____ Miles/Time _____

Notes _____

Thursday   Date

Swim _____

_____ Yards _____

Bike _____

_____ Miles/Time _____

Run _____

_____ Miles/Time _____

Notes _____

Friday
Date

Swim _____
_____ Yards _____

Bike _____
_____ Miles/Time _____

Run _____
_____ Miles/Time _____

Notes _____

Saturday
Date

Swim _____
_____ Yards _____

Bike _____
_____ Miles/Time _____

Run _____
_____ Miles/Time _____

Notes _____

Sunday
Date

Swim _____
_____ Yards _____

Bike _____
_____ Miles/Time _____

Run _____
_____ Miles/Time _____

Notes _____

Review

Goals/Notes _____
_____
_____
_____

Swim Total	Bike Total	Run Total

Monday

Date _____

Swim _____

_____ Yards _____

Bike _____

_____ Miles/Time _____

Run _____

_____ Miles/Time _____

Notes _____

Tuesday

Date _____

Swim _____

_____ Yards _____

Bike _____

_____ Miles/Time _____

Run _____

_____ Miles/Time _____

Notes _____

Wednesday

Date _____

Swim _____

_____ Yards _____

Bike _____

_____ Miles/Time _____

Run _____

_____ Miles/Time _____

Notes _____

Thursday

Date _____

Swim _____

_____ Yards _____

Bike _____

_____ Miles/Time _____

Run _____

_____ Miles/Time _____

Notes _____

Friday
Date

Swim _____
_____ Yards _____

Bike _____
_____ Miles/Time _____

Run _____
_____ Miles/Time _____

Notes _____

Saturday
Date

Swim _____
_____ Yards _____

Bike _____
_____ Miles/Time _____

Run _____
_____ Miles/Time _____

Notes _____

Sunday
Date

Swim _____
_____ Yards _____

Bike _____
_____ Miles/Time _____

Run _____
_____ Miles/Time _____

Notes _____

Review

Goals/Notes _____
_____
_____
_____
_____

Swim Total [   ]   **Bike Total** [   ]   **Run Total** [   ]

WEEK

17

Monday
Date _____

Swim _____
_____ Yards _____
Bike _____
_____ Miles/Time _____
Run _____
_____ Miles/Time _____
Notes _____

Tuesday
Date _____

Swim _____
_____ Yards _____
Bike _____
_____ Miles/Time _____
Run _____
_____ Miles/Time _____
Notes _____

Wednesday
Date _____

Swim _____
_____ Yards _____
Bike _____
_____ Miles/Time _____
Run _____
_____ Miles/Time _____
Notes _____

Thursday
Date _____

Swim _____
_____ Yards _____
Bike _____
_____ Miles/Time _____
Run _____
_____ Miles/Time _____
Notes _____

Friday

Date _____

Swim _____
_____ Yards _____

Bike _____
_____ Miles/Time _____

Run _____
_____ Miles/Time _____

Notes _____

Saturday

Date _____

Swim _____
_____ Yards _____

Bike _____
_____ Miles/Time _____

Run _____
_____ Miles/Time _____

Notes _____

Sunday

Date _____

Swim _____
_____ Yards _____

Bike _____
_____ Miles/Time _____

Run _____
_____ Miles/Time _____

Notes _____

Review

Goals/Notes _____
_____
_____
_____
_____

Swim Total [   ] **Bike Total** [   ] **Run Total** [   ]

Monday   Date

Swim _____

_____ Yards _____

Bike _____

_____ Miles/Time _____

Run _____

_____ Miles/Time _____

Notes _____

Tuesday   Date

Swim _____

_____ Yards _____

Bike _____

_____ Miles/Time _____

Run _____

_____ Miles/Time _____

Notes _____

Wednesday   Date

Swim _____

_____ Yards _____

Bike _____

_____ Miles/Time _____

Run _____

_____ Miles/Time _____

Notes _____

Thursday   Date

Swim _____

_____ Yards _____

Bike _____

_____ Miles/Time _____

Run _____

_____ Miles/Time _____

Notes _____

Friday

Date _____

Swim _____
_____ Yards _____

Bike _____
_____ Miles/Time _____

Run _____
_____ Miles/Time _____

Notes _____

Saturday

Date _____

Swim _____
_____ Yards _____

Bike _____
_____ Miles/Time _____

Run _____
_____ Miles/Time _____

Notes _____

Sunday

Date _____

Swim _____
_____ Yards _____

Bike _____
_____ Miles/Time _____

Run _____
_____ Miles/Time _____

Notes _____

Review

Goals/Notes _____
_____
_____
_____
_____

Swim Total [____] **Bike Total** [____] **Run Total** [____]

WEEK 19

Monday
Date _____

Swim _____
_____ Yards _____
Bike _____
_____ Miles/Time _____
Run _____
_____ Miles/Time _____
Notes _____

Tuesday
Date _____

Swim _____
_____ Yards _____
Bike _____
_____ Miles/Time _____
Run _____
_____ Miles/Time _____
Notes _____

Wednesday
Date _____

Swim _____
_____ Yards _____
Bike _____
_____ Miles/Time _____
Run _____
_____ Miles/Time _____
Notes _____

Thursday
Date _____

Swim _____
_____ Yards _____
Bike _____
_____ Miles/Time _____
Run _____
_____ Miles/Time _____
Notes _____

Friday

Date _____

Swim _____

_____ Yards _____

Bike _____

_____ Miles/Time _____

Run _____

_____ Miles/Time _____

Notes _____

Saturday

Date _____

Swim _____

_____ Yards _____

Bike _____

_____ Miles/Time _____

Run _____

_____ Miles/Time _____

Notes _____

Sunday

Date _____

Swim _____

_____ Yards _____

Bike _____

_____ Miles/Time _____

Run _____

_____ Miles/Time _____

Notes _____

Review

Goals/Notes _____

_____

_____

_____

_____

Swim Total [ ]   **Bike Total** [ ]   **Run Total** [ ]

Monday
Date

Swim _____

_____ Yards _____

Bike _____

_____ Miles/Time _____

Run _____

_____ Miles/Time _____

Notes _____

Tuesday
Date

Swim _____

_____ Yards _____

Bike _____

_____ Miles/Time _____

Run _____

_____ Miles/Time _____

Notes _____

Wednesday
Date

Swim _____

_____ Yards _____

Bike _____

_____ Miles/Time _____

Run _____

_____ Miles/Time _____

Notes _____

Thursday
Date

Swim _____

_____ Yards _____

Bike _____

_____ Miles/Time _____

Run _____

_____ Miles/Time _____

Notes _____

Friday
Date

Swim _____
_____ Yards _____

Bike _____
_____ Miles/Time _____

Run _____
_____ Miles/Time _____

Notes _____

Saturday
Date

Swim _____
_____ Yards _____

Bike _____
_____ Miles/Time _____

Run _____
_____ Miles/Time _____

Notes _____

Sunday
Date

Swim _____
_____ Yards _____

Bike _____
_____ Miles/Time _____

Run _____
_____ Miles/Time _____

Notes _____

Review

Goals/Notes _____
_____
_____
_____
_____

Swim Total [____] **Bike Total** [____] **Run Total** [____]

Monday

Date _____

Swim _____

_____ Yards _____

Bike _____

_____ Miles/Time _____

Run _____

_____ Miles/Time _____

Notes _____

Tuesday

Date _____

Swim _____

_____ Yards _____

Bike _____

_____ Miles/Time _____

Run _____

_____ Miles/Time _____

Notes _____

Wednesday

Date _____

Swim _____

_____ Yards _____

Bike _____

_____ Miles/Time _____

Run _____

_____ Miles/Time _____

Notes _____

Thursday

Date _____

Swim _____

_____ Yards _____

Bike _____

_____ Miles/Time _____

Run _____

_____ Miles/Time _____

Notes _____

Friday

Date _____

Swim _____
_____ Yards _____

Bike _____
_____ Miles/Time _____

Run _____
_____ Miles/Time _____

Notes _____

Saturday

Date _____

Swim _____
_____ Yards _____

Bike _____
_____ Miles/Time _____

Run _____
_____ Miles/Time _____

Notes _____

Sunday

Date _____

Swim _____
_____ Yards _____

Bike _____
_____ Miles/Time _____

Run _____
_____ Miles/Time _____

Notes _____

Review

Goals/Notes _____
_____
_____
_____
_____

Swim Total [ ]   **Bike Total** [ ]   **Run Total** [ ]

On the run, Maui Xterra World Championship

"Obstacles are what you see when you take your eyes off the goal."

—Luis Escobar

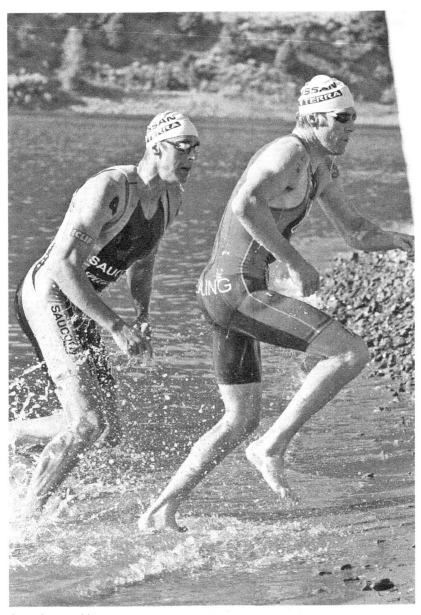

Competitors out of the water

"No pressure, no diamonds."

—Mary Case

Monday

Date _____

Swim _____

_____ Yards _____

Bike _____

_____ Miles/Time _____

Run _____

_____ Miles/Time _____

Notes _____

Tuesday

Date _____

Swim _____

_____ Yards _____

Bike _____

_____ Miles/Time _____

Run _____

_____ Miles/Time _____

Notes _____

Wednesday

Date _____

Swim _____

_____ Yards _____

Bike _____

_____ Miles/Time _____

Run _____

_____ Miles/Time _____

Notes _____

Thursday

Date _____

Swim _____

_____ Yards _____

Bike _____

_____ Miles/Time _____

Run _____

_____ Miles/Time _____

Notes _____

WEEK

22

Friday
Date _____

Swim _____
_____ Yards _____

Bike _____
_____ Miles/Time _____

Run _____
_____ Miles/Time _____

Notes _____

Saturday
Date _____

Swim _____
_____ Yards _____

Bike _____
_____ Miles/Time _____

Run _____
_____ Miles/Time _____

Notes _____

Sunday
Date _____

Swim _____
_____ Yards _____

Bike _____
_____ Miles/Time _____

Run _____
_____ Miles/Time _____

Notes _____

Review

Goals/Notes _____
_____
_____
_____
_____

Swim Total [ ]   **Bike Total** [ ]   **Run Total** [ ]

WEEK 23

Monday
Date _____

Swim _____

_____ Yards _____

Bike _____

_____ Miles/Time _____

Run _____

_____ Miles/Time _____

Notes _____

Tuesday
Date _____

Swim _____

_____ Yards _____

Bike _____

_____ Miles/Time _____

Run _____

_____ Miles/Time _____

Notes _____

Wednesday
Date _____

Swim _____

_____ Yards _____

Bike _____

_____ Miles/Time _____

Run _____

_____ Miles/Time _____

Notes _____

Thursday
Date _____

Swim _____

_____ Yards _____

Bike _____

_____ Miles/Time _____

Run _____

_____ Miles/Time _____

Notes _____

Friday
Date _____

Swim _____
_____ Yards _____

Bike _____
_____ Miles/Time _____

Run _____
_____ Miles/Time _____

Notes _____

Saturday
Date _____

Swim _____
_____ Yards _____

Bike _____
_____ Miles/Time _____

Run _____
_____ Miles/Time _____

Notes _____

Sunday
Date _____

Swim _____
_____ Yards _____

Bike _____
_____ Miles/Time _____

Run _____
_____ Miles/Time _____

Notes _____

Review

Goals/Notes _____
_____
_____
_____
_____

Swim Total [ ] Bike Total [ ] Run Total [ ]

WEEK
24

Monday
Date _____

Swim _____
_____ Yards _____
Bike _____
_____ Miles/Time _____
Run _____
_____ Miles/Time _____
Notes _____

Tuesday
Date _____

Swim _____
_____ Yards _____
Bike _____
_____ Miles/Time _____
Run _____
_____ Miles/Time _____
Notes _____

Wednesday
Date _____

Swim _____
_____ Yards _____
Bike _____
_____ Miles/Time _____
Run _____
_____ Miles/Time _____
Notes _____

Thursday
Date _____

Swim _____
_____ Yards _____
Bike _____
_____ Miles/Time _____
Run _____
_____ Miles/Time _____
Notes _____

Friday
Date _____

Swim _____
_____ Yards _____

Bike _____
_____ Miles/Time _____

Run _____
_____ Miles/Time _____

Notes _____

Saturday
Date _____

Swim _____
_____ Yards _____

Bike _____
_____ Miles/Time _____

Run _____
_____ Miles/Time _____

Notes _____

Sunday
Date _____

Swim _____
_____ Yards _____

Bike _____
_____ Miles/Time _____

Run _____
_____ Miles/Time _____

Notes _____

Review

Goals/Notes _____
_____
_____
_____
_____

Swim Total	Bike Total	Run Total

Monday

Date _____

Swim _____

_____ Yards _____

Bike _____

_____ Miles/Time _____

Run _____

_____ Miles/Time _____

Notes _____

Tuesday

Date _____

Swim _____

_____ Yards _____

Bike _____

_____ Miles/Time _____

Run _____

_____ Miles/Time _____

Notes _____

Wednesday

Date _____

Swim _____

_____ Yards _____

Bike _____

_____ Miles/Time _____

Run _____

_____ Miles/Time _____

Notes _____

Thursday

Date _____

Swim _____

_____ Yards _____

Bike _____

_____ Miles/Time _____

Run _____

_____ Miles/Time _____

Notes _____

Friday
Date _____

Swim _____
_____ Yards _____

Bike _____
_____ Miles/Time _____

Run _____
_____ Miles/Time _____

Notes _____

Saturday
Date _____

Swim _____
_____ Yards _____

Bike _____
_____ Miles/Time _____

Run _____
_____ Miles/Time _____

Notes _____

Sunday
Date _____

Swim _____
_____ Yards _____

Bike _____
_____ Miles/Time _____

Run _____
_____ Miles/Time _____

Notes _____

Review

Goals/Notes _____
_____
_____
_____
_____

Swim Total [ ]   **Bike Total** [ ]   **Run Total** [ ]

WEEK 26

Monday
Date

Swim _____

_____ Yards _____

Bike _____

_____ Miles/Time _____

Run _____

_____ Miles/Time _____

Notes _____

Tuesday
Date

Swim _____

_____ Yards _____

Bike _____

_____ Miles/Time _____

Run _____

_____ Miles/Time _____

Notes _____

Wednesday
Date

Swim _____

_____ Yards _____

Bike _____

_____ Miles/Time _____

Run _____

_____ Miles/Time _____

Notes _____

Thursday
Date

Swim _____

_____ Yards _____

Bike _____

_____ Miles/Time _____

Run _____

_____ Miles/Time _____

Notes _____

WEEK 26

Friday
Date _____

Swim _____
_____ Yards _____

Bike _____
_____ Miles/Time _____

Run _____
_____ Miles/Time _____

Notes _____

Saturday
Date _____

Swim _____
_____ Yards _____

Bike _____
_____ Miles/Time _____

Run _____
_____ Miles/Time _____

Notes _____

Sunday
Date _____

Swim _____
_____ Yards _____

Bike _____
_____ Miles/Time _____

Run _____
_____ Miles/Time _____

Notes _____

Review

Goals/Notes _____
_____
_____
_____
_____

Swim Total [____]   Bike Total [____]   Run Total [____]

Monday

Date _____

Swim _____

_____ Yards _____

Bike _____

_____ Miles/Time ___

Run _____

_____ Miles/Time ___

Notes _____

Tuesday

Date _____

Swim _____

_____ Yards _____

Bike _____

_____ Miles/Time ___

Run _____

_____ Miles/Time ___

Notes _____

Wednesday

Date _____

Swim _____

_____ Yards _____

Bike _____

_____ Miles/Time ___

Run _____

_____ Miles/Time ___

Notes _____

Thursday

Date _____

Swim _____

_____ Yards _____

Bike _____

_____ Miles/Time ___

Run _____

_____ Miles/Time ___

Notes _____

Friday   Date

Swim _____
_____ Yards _____

Bike _____
_____ Miles/Time _____

Run _____
_____ Miles/Time _____

Notes _____

Saturday   Date

Swim _____
_____ Yards _____

Bike _____
_____ Miles/Time _____

Run _____
_____ Miles/Time _____

Notes _____

Sunday   Date

Swim _____
_____ Yards _____

Bike _____
_____ Miles/Time _____

Run _____
_____ Miles/Time _____

Notes _____

Review

Goals/Notes _____
_____
_____
_____
_____

Swim Total [   ]   Bike Total [   ]   Run Total [   ]

Monday
Date

Swim _____
_____ Yards _____
Bike _____
_____ Miles/Time _____
Run _____
_____ Miles/Time _____
Notes _____

Tuesday
Date

Swim _____
_____ Yards _____
Bike _____
_____ Miles/Time _____
Run _____
_____ Miles/Time _____
Notes _____

Wednesday
Date

Swim _____
_____ Yards _____
Bike _____
_____ Miles/Time _____
Run _____
_____ Miles/Time _____
Notes _____

Thursday
Date

Swim _____
_____ Yards _____
Bike _____
_____ Miles/Time _____
Run _____
_____ Miles/Time _____
Notes _____

Friday _____ Date _____

Swim _____
_____ Yards _____

Bike _____
_____ Miles/Time _____

Run _____
_____ Miles/Time _____

Notes _____

Saturday _____ Date _____

Swim _____
_____ Yards _____

Bike _____
_____ Miles/Time _____

Run _____
_____ Miles/Time _____

Notes _____

Sunday _____ Date _____

Swim _____
_____ Yards _____

Bike _____
_____ Miles/Time _____

Run _____
_____ Miles/Time _____

Notes _____

Review _____

Goals/Notes _____
_____
_____
_____

Swim Total [____] Bike Total [____] Run Total [____]

Emma Snowsill, multiple ITU World Champion, on the bike, L.A. Triathlon

*"If you can't fly, then run. If you can't run, then walk.
If you can't walk, then crawl.
But whatever you do, keep moving."*

—Martin Luther King Jr.

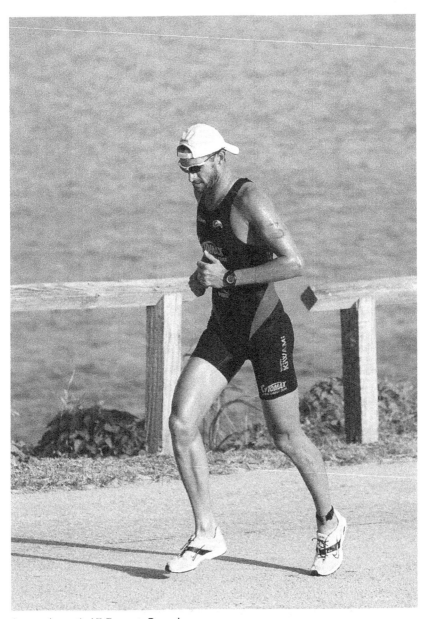

A competitor up the hill, Escape to Bermuda

*"Some of the world's greatest feats
were accomplished by people not smart enough
to know they were impossible."*
–Doug Larson

Monday   Date

Swim _____
_____ Yards _____
Bike _____
_____ Miles/Time _____
Run _____
_____ Miles/Time _____
Notes _____

Tuesday   Date

Swim _____
_____ Yards _____
Bike _____
_____ Miles/Time _____
Run _____
_____ Miles/Time _____
Notes _____

Wednesday   Date

Swim _____
_____ Yards _____
Bike _____
_____ Miles/Time _____
Run _____
_____ Miles/Time _____
Notes _____

Thursday   Date

Swim _____
_____ Yards _____
Bike _____
_____ Miles/Time _____
Run _____
_____ Miles/Time _____
Notes _____

Friday _____ Date _____

Swim _____
_____ Yards _____

Bike _____
_____ Miles/Time _____

Run _____
_____ Miles/Time _____

Notes _____

Saturday _____ Date _____

Swim _____
_____ Yards _____

Bike _____
_____ Miles/Time _____

Run _____
_____ Miles/Time _____

Notes _____

Sunday _____ Date _____

Swim _____
_____ Yards _____

Bike _____
_____ Miles/Time _____

Run _____
_____ Miles/Time _____

Notes _____

Review _____

Goals/Notes _____
_____
_____
_____
_____

Swim Total	Bike Total	Run Total

Monday

Date _____

Swim _____

_____ Yards _____

Bike _____

_____ Miles/Time _____

Run _____

_____ Miles/Time _____

Notes _____

Tuesday

Date _____

Swim _____

_____ Yards _____

Bike _____

_____ Miles/Time _____

Run _____

_____ Miles/Time _____

Notes _____

Wednesday

Date _____

Swim _____

_____ Yards _____

Bike _____

_____ Miles/Time _____

Run _____

_____ Miles/Time _____

Notes _____

Thursday

Date _____

Swim _____

_____ Yards _____

Bike _____

_____ Miles/Time _____

Run _____

_____ Miles/Time _____

Notes _____

Friday

Date _____

Swim _____
_____ Yards _____

Bike _____
_____ Miles/Time _____

Run _____
_____ Miles/Time _____

Notes _____

Saturday

Date _____

Swim _____
_____ Yards _____

Bike _____
_____ Miles/Time _____

Run _____
_____ Miles/Time _____

Notes _____

Sunday

Date _____

Swim _____
_____ Yards _____

Bike _____
_____ Miles/Time _____

Run _____
_____ Miles/Time _____

Notes _____

Review

Goals/Notes _____
_____
_____
_____
_____

Swim Total [   ]   **Bike Total** [   ]   **Run Total** [   ]

WEEK

31

Monday
Date _____

Swim _____
_____ Yards _____
Bike _____
_____ Miles/Time _____
Run _____
_____ Miles/Time _____
Notes _____

Tuesday
Date _____

Swim _____
_____ Yards _____
Bike _____
_____ Miles/Time _____
Run _____
_____ Miles/Time _____
Notes _____

Wednesday
Date _____

Swim _____
_____ Yards _____
Bike _____
_____ Miles/Time _____
Run _____
_____ Miles/Time _____
Notes _____

Thursday
Date _____

Swim _____
_____ Yards _____
Bike _____
_____ Miles/Time _____
Run _____
_____ Miles/Time _____
Notes _____

Friday   Date

Swim _____
_____ Yards _____

Bike _____
_____ Miles/Time _____

Run _____
_____ Miles/Time _____

Notes _____

Saturday   Date

Swim _____
_____ Yards _____

Bike _____
_____ Miles/Time _____

Run _____
_____ Miles/Time _____

Notes _____

Sunday   Date

Swim _____
_____ Yards _____

Bike _____
_____ Miles/Time _____

Run _____
_____ Miles/Time _____

Notes _____

Review

Goals/Notes _____
_____
_____
_____
_____

Swim Total [   ]   **Bike Total** [   ]   **Run Total** [   ]

WEEK 32

Monday
Date _____

Swim _____
_____ Yards _____
Bike _____
_____ Miles/Time _____
Run _____
_____ Miles/Time _____
Notes _____

Tuesday
Date _____

Swim _____
_____ Yards _____
Bike _____
_____ Miles/Time _____
Run _____
_____ Miles/Time _____
Notes _____

Wednesday
Date _____

Swim _____
_____ Yards _____
Bike _____
_____ Miles/Time _____
Run _____
_____ Miles/Time _____
Notes _____

Thursday
Date _____

Swim _____
_____ Yards _____
Bike _____
_____ Miles/Time _____
Run _____
_____ Miles/Time _____
Notes _____

Friday _____ Date _____

Swim _____
_____ Yards _____
Bike _____
_____ Miles/Time ____
Run _____
_____ Miles/Time ____
Notes _____

Saturday _____ Date _____

Swim _____
_____ Yards _____
Bike _____
_____ Miles/Time ____
Run _____
_____ Miles/Time ____
Notes _____

Sunday _____ Date _____

Swim _____
_____ Yards _____
Bike _____
_____ Miles/Time ____
Run _____
_____ Miles/Time ____
Notes _____

Review _____

Goals/Notes _____
_____
_____
_____
_____

Swim Total [   ] **Bike Total** [   ] **Run Total** [   ]

WEEK 33

Monday
Date _____

Swim _____
_____ Yards _____

Bike _____
_____ Miles/Time _____

Run _____
_____ Miles/Time _____

Notes _____

Tuesday
Date _____

Swim _____
_____ Yards _____

Bike _____
_____ Miles/Time _____

Run _____
_____ Miles/Time _____

Notes _____

Wednesday
Date _____

Swim _____
_____ Yards _____

Bike _____
_____ Miles/Time _____

Run _____
_____ Miles/Time _____

Notes _____

Thursday
Date _____

Swim _____
_____ Yards _____

Bike _____
_____ Miles/Time _____

Run _____
_____ Miles/Time _____

Notes _____

Friday

Date _____

Swim _____
_____ Yards _____
Bike _____
_____ Miles/Time _____
Run _____
_____ Miles/Time _____
Notes _____

Saturday

Date _____

Swim _____
_____ Yards _____
Bike _____
_____ Miles/Time _____
Run _____
_____ Miles/Time _____
Notes _____

Sunday

Date _____

Swim _____
_____ Yards _____
Bike _____
_____ Miles/Time _____
Run _____
_____ Miles/Time _____
Notes _____

Review

Goals/Notes _____
_____
_____
_____
_____

Swim Total	Bike Total	Run Total

Monday
Date _____

Swim _____
_____ Yards _____
Bike _____
_____ Miles/Time _____
Run _____
_____ Miles/Time _____
Notes _____

Tuesday
Date _____

Swim _____
_____ Yards _____
Bike _____
_____ Miles/Time _____
Run _____
_____ Miles/Time _____
Notes _____

Wednesday
Date _____

Swim _____
_____ Yards _____
Bike _____
_____ Miles/Time _____
Run _____
_____ Miles/Time _____
Notes _____

Thursday
Date _____

Swim _____
_____ Yards _____
Bike _____
_____ Miles/Time _____
Run _____
_____ Miles/Time _____
Notes _____

Friday

Date _____

Swim _____

_____ Yards _____

Bike _____

_____ Miles/Time _____

Run _____

_____ Miles/Time _____

Notes _____

Saturday

Date _____

Swim _____

_____ Yards _____

Bike _____

_____ Miles/Time _____

Run _____

_____ Miles/Time _____

Notes _____

Sunday

Date _____

Swim _____

_____ Yards _____

Bike _____

_____ Miles/Time _____

Run _____

_____ Miles/Time _____

Notes _____

Review

Goals/Notes _____

_____

_____

_____

Swim Total		Bike Total		Run Total	

Monday   Date

Swim _____
_____ Yards _____
Bike _____
_____ Miles/Time _____
Run _____
_____ Miles/Time _____
Notes _____

Tuesday   Date

Swim _____
_____ Yards _____
Bike _____
_____ Miles/Time _____
Run _____
_____ Miles/Time _____
Notes _____

Wednesday   Date

Swim _____
_____ Yards _____
Bike _____
_____ Miles/Time _____
Run _____
_____ Miles/Time _____
Notes _____

Thursday   Date

Swim _____
_____ Yards _____
Bike _____
_____ Miles/Time _____
Run _____
_____ Miles/Time _____
Notes _____

Friday

Date _____

Swim _____
_____ Yards _____
Bike _____
_____ Miles/Time _____
Run _____
_____ Miles/Time _____
Notes _____

Saturday

Date _____

Swim _____
_____ Yards _____
Bike _____
_____ Miles/Time _____
Run _____
_____ Miles/Time _____
Notes _____

Sunday

Date _____

Swim _____
_____ Yards _____
Bike _____
_____ Miles/Time _____
Run _____
_____ Miles/Time _____
Notes _____

Review

Goals/Notes _____
_____
_____
_____

Swim Total [_____]   **Bike Total** [_____]   **Run Total** [_____]

Candy Angle, former Xterra World Champion, out of the swim, Tahoe Xterra

*"Luck is where preparation
and opportunity meet."*

–Chinese proverb

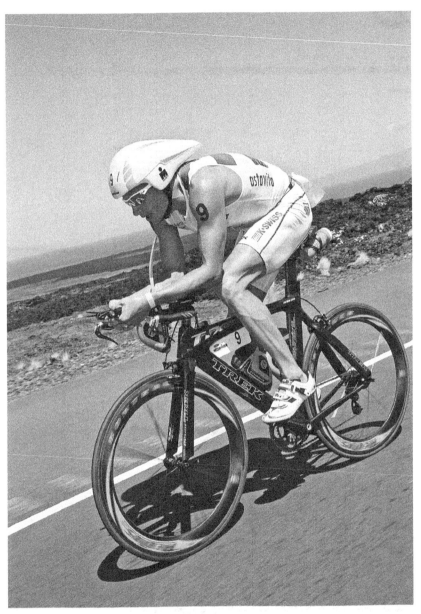

On the bike, Ford Ironman World Championship

"Nobody can prevent you
from choosing to be exceptional."

–Mark Sanborn

WEEK 36

Monday
Date _____

Swim _____
_____ Yards _____
Bike _____
_____ Miles/Time _____
Run _____
_____ Miles/Time _____
Notes _____

Tuesday
Date _____

Swim _____
_____ Yards _____
Bike _____
_____ Miles/Time _____
Run _____
_____ Miles/Time _____
Notes _____

Wednesday
Date _____

Swim _____
_____ Yards _____
Bike _____
_____ Miles/Time _____
Run _____
_____ Miles/Time _____
Notes _____

Thursday
Date _____

Swim _____
_____ Yards _____
Bike _____
_____ Miles/Time _____
Run _____
_____ Miles/Time _____
Notes _____

Friday
Date _____

Swim _____
_____ Yards _____

Bike _____
_____ Miles/Time _____

Run _____
_____ Miles/Time _____

Notes _____

Saturday
Date _____

Swim _____
_____ Yards _____

Bike _____
_____ Miles/Time _____

Run _____
_____ Miles/Time _____

Notes _____

Sunday
Date _____

Swim _____
_____ Yards _____

Bike _____
_____ Miles/Time _____

Run _____
_____ Miles/Time _____

Notes _____

Review

Goals/Notes _____
_____
_____
_____
_____

Swim Total [ ]   **Bike Total** [ ]   **Run Total** [ ]

Monday
Date _____

Swim _____

_____ Yards _____

Bike _____

_____ Miles/Time _____

Run _____

_____ Miles/Time _____

Notes _____

Tuesday
Date _____

Swim _____

_____ Yards _____

Bike _____

_____ Miles/Time _____

Run _____

_____ Miles/Time _____

Notes _____

Wednesday
Date _____

Swim _____

_____ Yards _____

Bike _____

_____ Miles/Time _____

Run _____

_____ Miles/Time _____

Notes _____

Thursday
Date _____

Swim _____

_____ Yards _____

Bike _____

_____ Miles/Time _____

Run _____

_____ Miles/Time _____

Notes _____

WEEK 37

Friday

Date

Swim

Yards

Bike

Miles/Time

Run

Miles/Time

Notes

Saturday

Date

Swim

Yards

Bike

Miles/Time

Run

Miles/Time

Notes

Sunday

Date

Swim

Yards

Bike

Miles/Time

Run

Miles/Time

Notes

Review

Goals/Notes

Swim Total

Bike Total

Run Total

Monday
Date

Swim _____
_____ Yards _____
Bike _____
_____ Miles/Time _____
Run _____
_____ Miles/Time _____
Notes _____

Tuesday
Date

Swim _____
_____ Yards _____
Bike _____
_____ Miles/Time _____
Run _____
_____ Miles/Time _____
Notes _____

Wednesday
Date

Swim _____
_____ Yards _____
Bike _____
_____ Miles/Time _____
Run _____
_____ Miles/Time _____
Notes _____

Thursday
Date

Swim _____
_____ Yards _____
Bike _____
_____ Miles/Time _____
Run _____
_____ Miles/Time _____
Notes _____

Friday

Date _____

Swim _____

_____ Yards _____

Bike _____

_____ Miles/Time _____

Run _____

_____ Miles/Time _____

Notes _____

Saturday

Date _____

Swim _____

_____ Yards _____

Bike _____

_____ Miles/Time _____

Run _____

_____ Miles/Time _____

Notes _____

Sunday

Date _____

Swim _____

_____ Yards _____

Bike _____

_____ Miles/Time _____

Run _____

_____ Miles/Time _____

Notes _____

Review

Goals/Notes _____

_____

_____

_____

_____

Swim Total [   ]   **Bike Total** [   ]   **Run Total** [   ]

Monday

Date _____

Swim _____
_____ Yards _____

Bike _____
_____ Miles/Time _____

Run _____
_____ Miles/Time _____

Notes _____

Tuesday

Date _____

Swim _____
_____ Yards _____

Bike _____
_____ Miles/Time _____

Run _____
_____ Miles/Time _____

Notes _____

Wednesday

Date _____

Swim _____
_____ Yards _____

Bike _____
_____ Miles/Time _____

Run _____
_____ Miles/Time _____

Notes _____

Thursday

Date _____

Swim _____
_____ Yards _____

Bike _____
_____ Miles/Time _____

Run _____
_____ Miles/Time _____

Notes _____

Friday
Date _____

Swim _____
_____ Yards _____

Bike _____
_____ Miles/Time ____

Run _____
_____ Miles/Time ____

Notes _____

Saturday
Date _____

Swim _____
_____ Yards _____

Bike _____
_____ Miles/Time ____

Run _____
_____ Miles/Time ____

Notes _____

Sunday
Date _____

Swim _____
_____ Yards _____

Bike _____
_____ Miles/Time ____

Run _____
_____ Miles/Time ____

Notes _____

Review

Goals/Notes _____
_____
_____
_____
_____

Swim Total [ ]   **Bike Total** [ ]   **Run Total** [ ]

Monday
Date _____

Swim _____
_____ Yards _____

Bike _____
_____ Miles/Time _____

Run _____
_____ Miles/Time _____

Notes _____

Tuesday
Date _____

Swim _____
_____ Yards _____

Bike _____
_____ Miles/Time _____

Run _____
_____ Miles/Time _____

Notes _____

Wednesday
Date _____

Swim _____
_____ Yards _____

Bike _____
_____ Miles/Time _____

Run _____
_____ Miles/Time _____

Notes _____

Thursday
Date _____

Swim _____
_____ Yards _____

Bike _____
_____ Miles/Time _____

Run _____
_____ Miles/Time _____

Notes _____

Friday
Date

Swim _____
_____ Yards _____
Bike _____
_____ Miles/Time _____
Run _____
_____ Miles/Time _____
Notes _____

Saturday
Date

Swim _____
_____ Yards _____
Bike _____
_____ Miles/Time _____
Run _____
_____ Miles/Time _____
Notes _____

Sunday
Date

Swim _____
_____ Yards _____
Bike _____
_____ Miles/Time _____
Run _____
_____ Miles/Time _____
Notes _____

Review

Goals/Notes _____
_____
_____
_____
_____

Swim Total [ ] **Bike Total** [ ] **Run Total** [ ]

Monday   Date

Swim _____
_____ Yards _____
Bike _____
_____ Miles/Time _____
Run _____
_____ Miles/Time _____
Notes _____

Tuesday   Date

Swim _____
_____ Yards _____
Bike _____
_____ Miles/Time _____
Run _____
_____ Miles/Time _____
Notes _____

Wednesday   Date

Swim _____
_____ Yards _____
Bike _____
_____ Miles/Time _____
Run _____
_____ Miles/Time _____
Notes _____

Thursday   Date

Swim _____
_____ Yards _____
Bike _____
_____ Miles/Time _____
Run _____
_____ Miles/Time _____
Notes _____

Friday
Date _____

Swim _____
_____ Yards _____
Bike _____
_____ Miles/Time _____
Run _____
_____ Miles/Time _____
Notes _____

Saturday
Date _____

Swim _____
_____ Yards _____
Bike _____
_____ Miles/Time _____
Run _____
_____ Miles/Time _____
Notes _____

Sunday
Date _____

Swim _____
_____ Yards _____
Bike _____
_____ Miles/Time _____
Run _____
_____ Miles/Time _____
Notes _____

Review

Goals/Notes _____
_____
_____
_____
_____

Swim Total		Bike Total		Run Total	

Monday
Date _____

Swim _____
_____ Yards _____
Bike _____
_____ Miles/Time _____
Run _____
_____ Miles/Time _____
Notes _____

Tuesday
Date _____

Swim _____
_____ Yards _____
Bike _____
_____ Miles/Time _____
Run _____
_____ Miles/Time _____
Notes _____

Wednesday
Date _____

Swim _____
_____ Yards _____
Bike _____
_____ Miles/Time _____
Run _____
_____ Miles/Time _____
Notes _____

Thursday
Date _____

Swim _____
_____ Yards _____
Bike _____
_____ Miles/Time _____
Run _____
_____ Miles/Time _____
Notes _____

Friday   Date

Swim _____
_____ Yards _____

Bike _____
_____ Miles/Time _____

Run _____
_____ Miles/Time _____

Notes _____

Saturday   Date

Swim _____
_____ Yards _____

Bike _____
_____ Miles/Time _____

Run _____
_____ Miles/Time _____

Notes _____

Sunday   Date

Swim _____
_____ Yards _____

Bike _____
_____ Miles/Time _____

Run _____
_____ Miles/Time _____

Notes _____

Review

Goals/Notes _____
_____
_____
_____

Swim Total [____]   **Bike Total** [____]   **Run Total** [____]

Pushing the bike up Heartbreak Hill, Maui Xterra World Championship

"Do or do not. There is no try."

−Yoda

Crossing the finish line, Ironman, Kona, Hawaii

"Only dreamers can teach us to soar."

–Anne Marie Pierce

WEEK 43

Monday
Date _____

Swim _____
_____ Yards _____
Bike _____
_____ Miles/Time _____
Run _____
_____ Miles/Time _____
Notes _____

Tuesday
Date _____

Swim _____
_____ Yards _____
Bike _____
_____ Miles/Time _____
Run _____
_____ Miles/Time _____
Notes _____

Wednesday
Date _____

Swim _____
_____ Yards _____
Bike _____
_____ Miles/Time _____
Run _____
_____ Miles/Time _____
Notes _____

Thursday
Date _____

Swim _____
_____ Yards _____
Bike _____
_____ Miles/Time _____
Run _____
_____ Miles/Time _____
Notes _____

Friday
Date

Swim _____
_____ Yards _____

Bike _____
_____ Miles/Time _____

Run _____
_____ Miles/Time _____

Notes _____

Saturday
Date

Swim _____
_____ Yards _____

Bike _____
_____ Miles/Time _____

Run _____
_____ Miles/Time _____

Notes _____

Sunday
Date

Swim _____
_____ Yards _____

Bike _____
_____ Miles/Time _____

Run _____
_____ Miles/Time _____

Notes _____

Review

Goals/Notes _____
_____
_____
_____

Swim Total [ ] **Bike Total** [ ] **Run Total** [ ]

WEEK 44

Monday
Date _____

Swim _____
_____ Yards _____

Bike _____
_____ Miles/Time _____

Run _____
_____ Miles/Time _____

Notes _____

Tuesday
Date _____

Swim _____
_____ Yards _____

Bike _____
_____ Miles/Time _____

Run _____
_____ Miles/Time _____

Notes _____

Wednesday
Date _____

Swim _____
_____ Yards _____

Bike _____
_____ Miles/Time _____

Run _____
_____ Miles/Time _____

Notes _____

Thursday
Date _____

Swim _____
_____ Yards _____

Bike _____
_____ Miles/Time _____

Run _____
_____ Miles/Time _____

Notes _____

Friday

Date _____

Swim _____
_____ Yards _____
Bike _____
_____ Miles/Time _____
Run _____
_____ Miles/Time _____
Notes _____

Saturday

Date _____

Swim _____
_____ Yards _____
Bike _____
_____ Miles/Time _____
Run _____
_____ Miles/Time _____
Notes _____

Sunday

Date _____

Swim _____
_____ Yards _____
Bike _____
_____ Miles/Time _____
Run _____
_____ Miles/Time _____
Notes _____

Review

Goals/Notes _____
_____
_____
_____
_____

Swim Total [____]   **Bike Total** [____]   **Run Total** [____]

Monday

Date _____

Swim _____
_____ Yards _____
Bike _____
_____ Miles/Time _____
Run _____
_____ Miles/Time _____
Notes _____

Tuesday

Date _____

Swim _____
_____ Yards _____
Bike _____
_____ Miles/Time _____
Run _____
_____ Miles/Time _____
Notes _____

Wednesday

Date _____

Swim _____
_____ Yards _____
Bike _____
_____ Miles/Time _____
Run _____
_____ Miles/Time _____
Notes _____

Thursday

Date _____

Swim _____
_____ Yards _____
Bike _____
_____ Miles/Time _____
Run _____
_____ Miles/Time _____
Notes _____

Friday

Date _____

Swim _____

_____ Yards _____

Bike _____

_____ Miles/Time _____

Run _____

_____ Miles/Time _____

Notes _____

Saturday

Date _____

Swim _____

_____ Yards _____

Bike _____

_____ Miles/Time _____

Run _____

_____ Miles/Time _____

Notes _____

Sunday

Date _____

Swim _____

_____ Yards _____

Bike _____

_____ Miles/Time _____

Run _____

_____ Miles/Time _____

Notes _____

Review

Goals/Notes _____

_____

_____

_____

Swim Total	Bike Total	Run Total

Monday
Date _____

Swim _____
_____ Yards _____
Bike _____
_____ Miles/Time _____
Run _____
_____ Miles/Time _____
Notes _____

Tuesday
Date _____

Swim _____
_____ Yards _____
Bike _____
_____ Miles/Time _____
Run _____
_____ Miles/Time _____
Notes _____

Wednesday
Date _____

Swim _____
_____ Yards _____
Bike _____
_____ Miles/Time _____
Run _____
_____ Miles/Time _____
Notes _____

Thursday
Date _____

Swim _____
_____ Yards _____
Bike _____
_____ Miles/Time _____
Run _____
_____ Miles/Time _____
Notes _____

Friday
Date _____

Swim _____
_____ Yards _____

Bike _____
_____ Miles/Time _____

Run _____
_____ Miles/Time _____

Notes _____

Saturday
Date _____

Swim _____
_____ Yards _____

Bike _____
_____ Miles/Time _____

Run _____
_____ Miles/Time _____

Notes _____

Sunday
Date _____

Swim _____
_____ Yards _____

Bike _____
_____ Miles/Time _____

Run _____
_____ Miles/Time _____

Notes _____

Review

Goals/Notes _____
_____
_____
_____
_____

Swim Total _____ **Bike Total** _____ **Run Total** _____

WEEK 47

Monday
Date _____

Swim _____
_____ Yards _____

Bike _____
_____ Miles/Time _____

Run _____
_____ Miles/Time _____

Notes _____

Tuesday
Date _____

Swim _____
_____ Yards _____

Bike _____
_____ Miles/Time _____

Run _____
_____ Miles/Time _____

Notes _____

Wednesday
Date _____

Swim _____
_____ Yards _____

Bike _____
_____ Miles/Time _____

Run _____
_____ Miles/Time _____

Notes _____

Thursday
Date _____

Swim _____
_____ Yards _____

Bike _____
_____ Miles/Time _____

Run _____
_____ Miles/Time _____

Notes _____

Friday

Date _____

Swim _____

_____ Yards _____

Bike _____

_____ Miles/Time _____

Run _____

_____ Miles/Time _____

Notes _____

Saturday

Date _____

Swim _____

_____ Yards _____

Bike _____

_____ Miles/Time _____

Run _____

_____ Miles/Time _____

Notes _____

Sunday

Date _____

Swim _____

_____ Yards _____

Bike _____

_____ Miles/Time _____

Run _____

_____ Miles/Time _____

Notes _____

Review

Goals/Notes _____

_____

_____

_____

_____

Swim Total	Bike Total	Run Total

WEEK 48

Monday
Date _____

Swim _____
_____ Yards _____

Bike _____
_____ Miles/Time _____

Run _____
_____ Miles/Time _____

Notes _____

Tuesday
Date _____

Swim _____
_____ Yards _____

Bike _____
_____ Miles/Time _____

Run _____
_____ Miles/Time _____

Notes _____

Wednesday
Date _____

Swim _____
_____ Yards _____

Bike _____
_____ Miles/Time _____

Run _____
_____ Miles/Time _____

Notes _____

Thursday
Date _____

Swim _____
_____ Yards _____

Bike _____
_____ Miles/Time _____

Run _____
_____ Miles/Time _____

Notes _____

Friday

Date _____

Swim _____
_____ Yards _____
Bike _____
_____ Miles/Time ____
Run _____
_____ Miles/Time ____
Notes _____

Saturday

Date _____

Swim _____
_____ Yards _____
Bike _____
_____ Miles/Time ____
Run _____
_____ Miles/Time ____
Notes _____

Sunday

Date _____

Swim _____
_____ Yards _____
Bike _____
_____ Miles/Time ____
Run _____
_____ Miles/Time ____
Notes _____

Review

Goals/Notes _____
_____
_____
_____
_____

Swim Total [____] **Bike Total** [____] **Run Total** [____]

WEEK 49

Monday
Date _____

Swim _____
_____ Yards _____
Bike _____
_____ Miles/Time _____
Run _____
_____ Miles/Time _____
Notes _____

Tuesday
Date _____

Swim _____
_____ Yards _____
Bike _____
_____ Miles/Time _____
Run _____
_____ Miles/Time _____
Notes _____

Wednesday
Date _____

Swim _____
_____ Yards _____
Bike _____
_____ Miles/Time _____
Run _____
_____ Miles/Time _____
Notes _____

Thursday
Date _____

Swim _____
_____ Yards _____
Bike _____
_____ Miles/Time _____
Run _____
_____ Miles/Time _____
Notes _____

Friday

Date _____

Swim _____
_____ Yards _____

Bike _____
_____ Miles/Time _____

Run _____
_____ Miles/Time _____

Notes _____

Saturday

Date _____

Swim _____
_____ Yards _____

Bike _____
_____ Miles/Time _____

Run _____
_____ Miles/Time _____

Notes _____

Sunday

Date _____

Swim _____
_____ Yards _____

Bike _____
_____ Miles/Time _____

Run _____
_____ Miles/Time _____

Notes _____

Review

Goals/Notes _____
_____
_____
_____
_____

Swim Total [   ]   **Bike Total** [   ]   **Run Total** [   ]

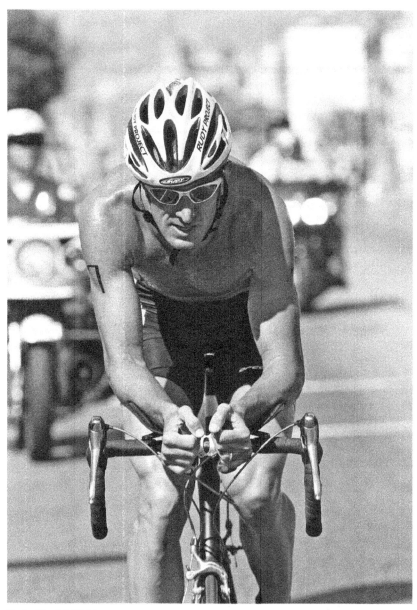

On the bike, L.A. Triathlon

"If you undertrain, you may not finish,
but if you overtrain, you may not start."

−Stan Jensen

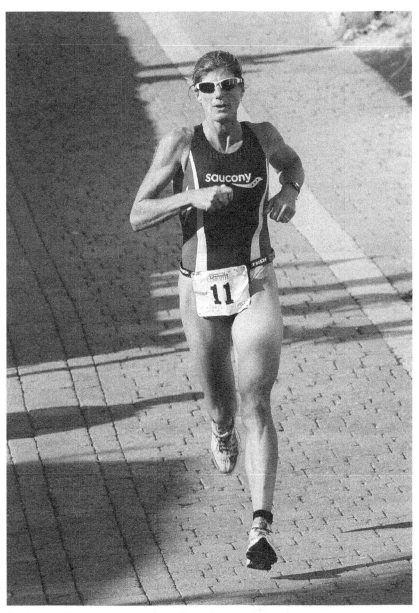

Running down the cobblestones, Escape to Bermuda

"I dream my painting and then paint my dream."
—*Vincent Van Gogh*

WEEK 50

Monday
Date _____

Swim _____
_____ Yards _____
Bike _____
_____ Miles/Time _____
Run _____
_____ Miles/Time _____
Notes _____

Tuesday
Date _____

Swim _____
_____ Yards _____
Bike _____
_____ Miles/Time _____
Run _____
_____ Miles/Time _____
Notes _____

Wednesday
Date _____

Swim _____
_____ Yards _____
Bike _____
_____ Miles/Time _____
Run _____
_____ Miles/Time _____
Notes _____

Thursday
Date _____

Swim _____
_____ Yards _____
Bike _____
_____ Miles/Time _____
Run _____
_____ Miles/Time _____
Notes _____

Friday   Date

Swim _____
_____ Yards _____

Bike _____
_____ Miles/Time _____

Run _____
_____ Miles/Time _____

Notes _____

Saturday   Date

Swim _____
_____ Yards _____

Bike _____
_____ Miles/Time _____

Run _____
_____ Miles/Time _____

Notes _____

Sunday   Date

Swim _____
_____ Yards _____

Bike _____
_____ Miles/Time _____

Run _____
_____ Miles/Time _____

Notes _____

Review

Goals/Notes _____
_____
_____
_____
_____

Swim Total [   ]   **Bike Total** [   ]   **Run Total** [   ]

WEEK 51

Monday
Date _____

Swim _____
_____ Yards _____
Bike _____
_____ Miles/Time _____
Run _____
_____ Miles/Time _____
Notes _____

Tuesday
Date _____

Swim _____
_____ Yards _____
Bike _____
_____ Miles/Time _____
Run _____
_____ Miles/Time _____
Notes _____

Wednesday
Date _____

Swim _____
_____ Yards _____
Bike _____
_____ Miles/Time _____
Run _____
_____ Miles/Time _____
Notes _____

Thursday
Date _____

Swim _____
_____ Yards _____
Bike _____
_____ Miles/Time _____
Run _____
_____ Miles/Time _____
Notes _____

Friday   Date

Swim _____
_____ Yards _____
Bike _____
_____ Miles/Time _____
Run _____
_____ Miles/Time _____
Notes _____

Saturday   Date

Swim _____
_____ Yards _____
Bike _____
_____ Miles/Time _____
Run _____
_____ Miles/Time _____
Notes _____

Sunday   Date

Swim _____
_____ Yards _____
Bike _____
_____ Miles/Time _____
Run _____
_____ Miles/Time _____
Notes _____

Review

Goals/Notes _____
_____
_____
_____

Swim Total [____]   **Bike Total** [____]   **Run Total** [____]

Monday
Date

Swim _____
_____ Yards _____
Bike _____
_____ Miles/Time _____
Run _____
_____ Miles/Time _____
Notes _____

Tuesday
Date

Swim _____
_____ Yards _____
Bike _____
_____ Miles/Time _____
Run _____
_____ Miles/Time _____
Notes _____

Wednesday
Date

Swim _____
_____ Yards _____
Bike _____
_____ Miles/Time _____
Run _____
_____ Miles/Time _____
Notes _____

Thursday
Date

Swim _____
_____ Yards _____
Bike _____
_____ Miles/Time _____
Run _____
_____ Miles/Time _____
Notes _____

Friday   Date

Swim _____

_____ Yards _____

Bike _____

_____ Miles/Time _____

Run _____

_____ Miles/Time _____

Notes _____

Saturday   Date

Swim _____

_____ Yards _____

Bike _____

_____ Miles/Time _____

Run _____

_____ Miles/Time _____

Notes _____

Sunday   Date

Swim _____

_____ Yards _____

Bike _____

_____ Miles/Time _____

Run _____

_____ Miles/Time _____

Notes _____

Review

Goals/Notes _____

_____

_____

_____

_____

Swim Total [   ]   **Bike Total** [   ]   **Run Total** [   ]

Monday
Date _____

Swim _____
_____ Yards _____

Bike _____
_____ Miles/Time _____

Run _____
_____ Miles/Time _____

Notes _____

Tuesday
Date _____

Swim _____
_____ Yards _____

Bike _____
_____ Miles/Time _____

Run _____
_____ Miles/Time _____

Notes _____

Wednesday
Date _____

Swim _____
_____ Yards _____

Bike _____
_____ Miles/Time _____

Run _____
_____ Miles/Time _____

Notes _____

Thursday
Date _____

Swim _____
_____ Yards _____

Bike _____
_____ Miles/Time _____

Run _____
_____ Miles/Time _____

Notes _____

Friday
Date

Swim _____

_____ Yards _____

Bike _____

_____ Miles/Time _____

Run _____

_____ Miles/Time _____

Notes _____

Saturday
Date

Swim _____

_____ Yards _____

Bike _____

_____ Miles/Time _____

Run _____

_____ Miles/Time _____

Notes _____

Sunday
Date

Swim _____

_____ Yards _____

Bike _____

_____ Miles/Time _____

Run _____

_____ Miles/Time _____

Notes _____

Review

Goals/Notes _____

_____

_____

_____

_____

Swim Total		**Bike Total**		**Run Total**	

Monday _____ Date _____

Swim _____
_____ Yards _____
Bike _____
_____ Miles/Time _____
Run _____
_____ Miles/Time _____
Notes _____

Tuesday _____ Date _____

Swim _____
_____ Yards _____
Bike _____
_____ Miles/Time _____
Run _____
_____ Miles/Time _____
Notes _____

Wednesday _____ Date _____

Swim _____
_____ Yards _____
Bike _____
_____ Miles/Time _____
Run _____
_____ Miles/Time _____
Notes _____

Thursday _____ Date _____

Swim _____
_____ Yards _____
Bike _____
_____ Miles/Time _____
Run _____
_____ Miles/Time _____
Notes _____

Friday
Date _____

Swim _____
_____ Yards _____

Bike _____
_____ Miles/Time _____

Run _____
_____ Miles/Time _____

Notes _____

Saturday
Date _____

Swim _____
_____ Yards _____

Bike _____
_____ Miles/Time _____

Run _____
_____ Miles/Time _____

Notes _____

Sunday
Date _____

Swim _____
_____ Yards _____

Bike _____
_____ Miles/Time _____

Run _____
_____ Miles/Time _____

Notes _____

Review
Goals/Notes _____
_____
_____
_____
_____

Swim Total [____] **Bike Total** [____] **Run Total** [____]

WEEK 55

Monday
Date _____

Swim _____

_____ Yards _____

Bike _____

_____ Miles/Time _____

Run _____

_____ Miles/Time _____

Notes _____

Tuesday
Date _____

Swim _____

_____ Yards _____

Bike _____

_____ Miles/Time _____

Run _____

_____ Miles/Time _____

Notes _____

Wednesday
Date _____

Swim _____

_____ Yards _____

Bike _____

_____ Miles/Time _____

Run _____

_____ Miles/Time _____

Notes _____

Thursday
Date _____

Swim _____

_____ Yards _____

Bike _____

_____ Miles/Time _____

Run _____

_____ Miles/Time _____

Notes _____

Friday   Date

Swim _____
_____ Yards _____

Bike _____
_____ Miles/Time _____

Run _____
_____ Miles/Time _____

Notes _____

Saturday   Date

Swim _____
_____ Yards _____

Bike _____
_____ Miles/Time _____

Run _____
_____ Miles/Time _____

Notes _____

Sunday   Date

Swim _____
_____ Yards _____

Bike _____
_____ Miles/Time _____

Run _____
_____ Miles/Time _____

Notes _____

Review

Goals/Notes _____
_____
_____
_____
_____

Swim Total		Bike Total		Run Total	

WEEK 56

Monday

Date _____

Swim _____

_____ Yards _____

Bike _____

_____ Miles/Time _____

Run _____

_____ Miles/Time _____

Notes _____

Tuesday

Date _____

Swim _____

_____ Yards _____

Bike _____

_____ Miles/Time _____

Run _____

_____ Miles/Time _____

Notes _____

Wednesday

Date _____

Swim _____

_____ Yards _____

Bike _____

_____ Miles/Time _____

Run _____

_____ Miles/Time _____

Notes _____

Thursday

Date _____

Swim _____

_____ Yards _____

Bike _____

_____ Miles/Time _____

Run _____

_____ Miles/Time _____

Notes _____

Friday

Date _____

Swim _____
_____ Yards _____

Bike _____
_____ Miles/Time _____

Run _____
_____ Miles/Time _____

Notes _____

Saturday

Date _____

Swim _____
_____ Yards _____

Bike _____
_____ Miles/Time _____

Run _____
_____ Miles/Time _____

Notes _____

Sunday

Date _____

Swim _____
_____ Yards _____

Bike _____
_____ Miles/Time _____

Run _____
_____ Miles/Time _____

Notes _____

Review

Goals/Notes _____
_____
_____
_____
_____

Swim Total [_____]   Bike Total [_____]   Run Total [_____]

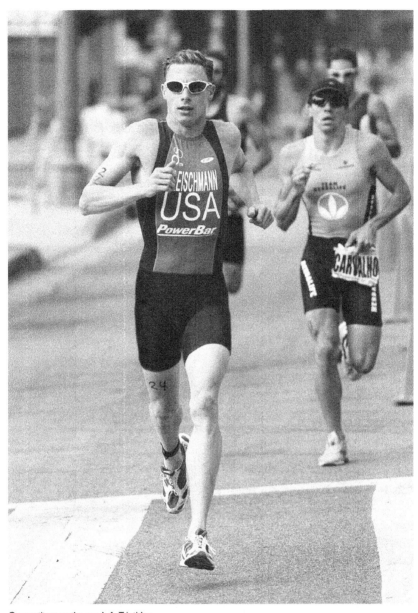

Competitors on the run, L.A. Triathlon

"May your mind soar and your pants always fit."
—Unknown

Additional Resources

*T*his training guide offers an introductory level of tips and workouts to help you get more out of your training. Consider the following books and other sources for more in-depth training discussions.

Books

Cycling

Allen, Hunter, and Andrew Coggan. *Training and Racing with a Power Meter*. Boulder, CO: VeloPress, 2006.

Edwards, Sally, and Sally Reed. *Heart Zones Cycling: The Avid Cyclist's Guide to Riding Faster and Farther*. Boulder, CO: VeloPress, 2006.

Hewitt, Ben. *Bicycling Magazine's Complete Book of Road Cycling Skills: Your Guide to Riding Faster, Stronger, Longer, and Safer*. Emmaus, PA: Rodale Books, 1998.

Nutrition

Applegate, Liz. *Encyclopedia of Sports and Fitness Nutrition*. New York: Prima Lifestyles, 2002.

Clark, Nancy. *Nancy Clark's Food Guide for Marathoners*. West Newton, MA: Sports Nutrition Publishers, 2002.

Clark, Nancy. *Nancy Clark's Sports Nutrition Guidebook*, 3rd ed. Champaign, IL: Human Kinetics, 2003.

Gastelu, Daniel, and Fred Hatfield. *Dynamic Nutrition for Maximum Performance: A Complete Nutritional Guide for Peak Sports Performance*. New York: Avery Publishing Group, 1997.

Hatfield, Fredrick C. *Nature's Sports Pharmacy*. New York: McGraw-Hill, 1999

Netzer, Corinne T. *The Complete Book of Food Counts*, 6th ed. New York: Dell, 2003.

Running

Kowalchik, Claire. *The Complete Book of Running for Women.*
New York: Pocket, 1999.

Glover, Bob, and Shelly-Lynn Florence Glover. *The Competitive
Runner's Handbook: The Bestselling Guide to Running 5Ks
Through Marathons.* New York: Penguin Books, 1999.

Higdon, Hal. *Marathon: The Ultimate Training Guide.* Emmaus,
PA: Rodale Books, 1999.

Swimming

Laughlin, Terry. *Triathlon Swimming Made Easy: The Total
Immersion Way for Anyone to Master Open-Water Swimming.*
New Paltz, NY: Total Immersion, 2004.

Laughlin, Terry, and John Delves. *Total Immersion: The
Revolutionary Way to Swim Better, Faster, and Easier.* New
York: Fireside, 1996.

Triathlon and Cross Training

Baechle, Thomas R., and Barney R. Groves. *Weight Training:
Steps to Success.* Champaign, IL: Human Kinetics, 2007.

Bernhardt, Gale. *Training Plans for Multisport Athletes: Your
Essential Guide to Triathlon, Duathlon, XTERRA, Ironman,
and Endurance Racing.* Boulder, CO: VeloPress, 2007.

Fahey, Thomas D. *Weight Training Basics.* New York: McGraw-
Hill, 2005.

Fitzgerald, Matt. *Triathlete Magazine's Complete Triathlon Book:
The Training, Diet, Health, Equipment, and Safety Tips You
Need to Do Your Best.* New York: Warner Books, 2003.

Friel, Joe. *The Triathlete's Training Bible*, 2nd ed. Boulder, CO:
VeloPress, 2004.

Friel, Joe. *Your First Triathlon.* Boulder, CO: VeloPress, 2006.

Harr, Eric. *Triathlon Training in Four Hours a Week.* Emmaus,
PA: Rodale Press, 2003.

Katai, Steve, and Colin Barr. *The Complete Idiot's Guide to
Triathlon Training.* New York: Alpha, 2007.

Williams, Jayne. *Slow Fat Triathlete: Live Your Athletic Dreams in
the Body You Have Now.* New York: Marlowe & Company, 2004.

Periodicals and Internet Resources

Competitor Magazine, competitor.com
> A long-standing magazine with several regional editions and website. It provides great connections to local events and races.

Cross Country Journal (CCJ), ccjournal.com
> Written for coaches, this bimonthly journal is devoted exclusively to cross-country running and coaching.

duathlon.com
> A unique website focused solely on duathlon, it includes race details and results as well as community information, photos, and classifieds.

Extreme Tri Magazine, xtri.com
> A triathlon-focused website with more than 1,600 how-to articles emphasizing advanced triathletes and longer races.

Inside Triathlon, insidetri.com
> A triathlon magazine and website with training resources and race information.

Runner's World, runnersworld.com
> The granddaddy of running magazines (and corresponding website), geared to a broad spectrum of running abilities and interests, with training articles, race information, results, and running news.

Running Times, runningtimes.com
> A long-standing magazine (and corresponding website) focused on running training tips, race results, and running news.

Trail Runner, trailrunnermag.com
> A running magazine and website focused on off-road running news, tips, events, and results.

Triathlete, triathletemag.com
> The granddaddy of triathlon magazines (and corresponding website), focused on triathlon training, events, results, and equipment.

triathlonweek.com
> A triathlon website focused on training articles, forums, and equipment.

About the Author

A competitive swimmer, runner, and triathlete, Tim Houts has authored six fitness books with more than 200,000 copies in print for triathlon, running, strength training, and more.

Tim swam competitively beginning in grade school and went on to play water polo at Stanford University. Since college, he has run three marathons, numerous 10Ks, and countless triathlons.

Share Your Comments at sportslog.com

If you'd like to share your comments about *TriLog*, we'd love to hear 'em. Let us know what you like best (and least). We can't promise to include all your suggestions, but we do promise to listen. Thanks!